mys·ti·cism

ˈmistəˌsizəm/

noun: *belief that union with or absorption into the Deity or the absolute, or the spiritual apprehension of knowledge inaccessible to the intellect, may be attained through contemplation and self-surrender*

Published by Pure Life Publishing

Plymouth, NH

copyright 2015

ISBN 978-1-329-46191-8

Cover Photo used with permission from

Charles Boumiea

Esalon Photography

I Know the Way You Can Get

I know the way you can get
When you have not had a drink of Love:

Your face hardens,
Your sweet muscles cramp.
Children become concerned
About a strange look that appears in your eyes
Which even begins to worry your own mirror
And nose.

Squirrels and birds sense your sadness
And call an important conference in a tall tree.
They decide which secret code to chant
To help your mind and soul.

Even angels fear that brand of madness
That arrays itself against the world
And throws sharp stones and spears into
The innocent
And into one's self.

O I know the way you can get
If you have not been drinking Love:

You might rip apart
Every sentence your friends and teachers say.
Looking for hidden clauses.

You might weigh every word on a scale
Like a dead fish.

You might pull out a ruler to measure
From every angle in your darkness
The beautiful dimensions of a heart you once
Trusted.

I know the way you can get
If you have not had a drink from Love's
Hands.

That is why all the Great Ones speak of
The vital need
To keep remembering God,
So you will come to know and see Him
As being Playful

And wanting,
Just Wanting to help.

That is why Hafiz says:
Bring your cup near me.
For all I care about
Is quenching your thirst for freedom!

All a Sane man can ever care about
Is giving Love!

~from 'I Heard God Laughing: Renderings of Hafiz'

Preface

Reverend Mary Francis pours out her great heart, her passionate spirit and her deep and enduring dedication to God, to life and to service in the poems and chapters of this uplifting and inspiring book. Having known the author for two decades, I can attest to the authenticity of her wisdom and the expansiveness of her heart. This is a true priest, one who has experienced the heights of heaven and the depths of hell on earth, and has emerged from both without losing her faith, her heart, her love of service and her passion for life. Her words will certainly light the way and lift the hearts of all who open to her wisdom and to her joy.

~Mother Clare Watts
author of Giving Birth to God:
A Woman's Path to Enlightenment &
Mystical Roses of Peace

TABLE OF CONTENTS

Section III: Peace

Section IV: Poetry by Rev Mary Francis Drake
(repeated in order of appearance)

Section IV: Poetry by Rev Mary Francis Drake
(cont.)

What to say

My heart yearns to share truth, to awaken hearts
What to say
Words like rivers flow from the minds and pens of the
ages
What more to say
Sounding the call of the spirit again in this age,
through this mind, with this pen
What left to say

Drunk on the sweetness of being
Love, clear and present
Breath, soft and rhythmic
Skin, alive and perceptive

What is that other we call life
That race, that mask, that noise
Deep silence drowns it out
Leaving depth without sound
Feeling without pretense
Heart without guards, without guile
Sweet tears of relief and joy
Simpleton at peace
Say that.

Introduction: This much I know is true….

I toyed with writing for many years before I started this effort. Having read libraries full of nonfiction related to psychology, science, spirituality, religion and mysticism, I felt that I didn't really have much to add to the many wonderful books that have helped to form me into who I am today. *'There's nothing new under the sun.'* That's what I told myself. And then I wondered to myself why so many people feel compelled to write about life and love from their perspective. Although not all of the books I have read have been life changing for me, each worked like water on a stone to soften, refine and shape me. Likewise, every person I meet has a similar impact. The beautiful dance of life…and the beautiful power of words that can continue to influence and inspire even after our spirits have long since departed this incarnation.

I don't pretend to know all of the mysteries of life and God, but I do know what I know….this much I know is true….that life and love have freed my heart from suffering and my soul from sin. As a Priest, this may be taken as a testimony of faith, but it is also a statement of trust…trust in the process of life and the unfolding consciousness in individual people and in humankind as a collective. At age 51, I find myself seeing a broader view, a deeper view, born of lost love, of betrayal, of grief, of grace, and of wonder. The beauties and joys of life are not lost on me, but neither are the pain and suffering, as I have endeavored to surrender to pain and dedicate myself to the alleviation of suffering in myself and the people that I encounter in my many roles in life....minister, counselor, teacher, hospice worker, mother, daughter, friend, colleague, human.

It is my hope and intention to offer some of the pearls of wisdom garnered from a half-century of living, loving and learning. My particular gems, in my unique voice; though they may be merely the echo of ages of wisdom and truth. I lend my voice, my experience, my heart to the pages and pages written before me for the upliftment of humankind and the glory of God.

Peace to you, and wonder,
Mary Francis Drake

SECTION I:

<u>THEORY</u>

It's All Good

Positive affirmations and wishful thinking aside, 'It's all good.' is a truth that reveals much about our state of being and approach to life. In its essence, it reveals that life is in support of life…in support of your life and my life, particularly, specifically, and universally. One could argue that 'bad' things happen and that's not 'good'….but if we look to the ancient truths of all philosophy, religion, spirituality and later psychology, we can see that karma is the balancing force of justice in the universe….regardless of one's particular belief system.

'You reap what you sow,' 'What goes around comes around,' 'They'll get theirs.' 'Do unto others….' No matter the tradition, as a collective humanity, we seem to know that what we put out will come back to us. If that's the case, and if the school of earth life is meant to teach us the highest of human values and qualities, then this return on our energetic and creative investment can be seen as an education rather than bad luck or victimization.

If it is, indeed, all good, then everything that comes into our lives comes to teach us about ourselves and about life. Whether we judge it as 'good' or 'bad' is really irrelevant, and only serves to intensify our pleasure or pain related to the experience rather than holding us accountable to the lesson at hand. As creative beings, our thoughts, words and actions create a sequence of events that will return to us at an undisclosed time, place and circumstance. We 'know not the hour' so the admonition of the major belief systems across time and culture tell us to prepare, keep our doorstep clean, and treat others the way we want to be treated.

If we are impatient to see the results of karma on our unkind or inconsiderate neighbors, then we are really just judging them and wanting to have them experience the pain that they are putting out by their 'bad' thoughts, words and deeds, on our timeline. This is not an altruistic approach to karma....it's actually just judgment in the guise of spirituality. If God, the Universe, Creation, Karma is the driving force of justice, what business have we in seeking to have front row seats as our 'enemies' get their comeuppance?

Really living with the 'It's all good' attitude requires acceptance, patience, trust and forbearance. It requires that we understand that a person who does negative or hurtful things will pay for those things and they will hurt because of them. In addition, it requires that we have mercy on the ignorance or pain that they carry around that would motivate such negativity.

As a student, follower and lover of Jesus, I look to his example to see how to approach such things. He tells us to love our enemies, to turn the other cheek, to forgive. Even more, He asks God to forgive those who have wrongly accused, beaten and crucified him by praying for them in saying, 'Father, forgive them, they know not what they do.' That's a high calling and a difficult example to follow. If we busy ourselves with working toward this type of response to the negative things that people say and do, we'll not have much time to judge or wish harm upon them.

The problem I see with the 'It's all good' slogan is that people apply it superficially and don't come to terms with the real harm that has been done to them so that they can feel, forgive and heal. Conversely people sometimes absolve themselves from having done harm by imagining that they are just part of the cosmic play of karma and that their hurtful/harmful deeds are all just 'a part of the big plan.' If we approach spiritual truths from a superficial perspective, we are simply repressing our feelings and experiences without validating them....dismissing them for some platitude that doesn't feed our soul. The result of this is a feeling of emptiness, loftiness, and eventually judgment over others as we struggle to keep our heads above water through spiritual comparison. This is a sad state of affairs. The one area of life that can actually transform us becomes relegated to a Pollyanna attitude of bubbles and butterflics that doesn't hold weight at the end of the day or at the end of our lives. This has sometimes been called 'spiritual bypassing' and it doesn't work any better than empty affirmations.

'It's all good' doesn't condone or dismiss negative behavior or experience....it explains it. From an eternal perspective, from a soul perspective, we are all learning to love one another and live in peace. While we are alive, we make mistakes and learn through the natural consequences that karma provides us. Sometimes we need 'sledge hammer' lessons to get our attention and teach us the basic truths of life and love. But when we attune ourselves to the universal, spiritual feedback loop that is karma, we can do the dance of life more gracefully and consciously, and we can clean up our messes as we go along.

God is kind and works on the competency model of education. If we are on our death bed and finally get it that we owe some people an apology and other people forgiveness, the burdens of karma can be dissipated in a few small acts of deep remorse and forgiveness. I have witnessed and experienced the miracle of this many times. The karmic record is changed and the resulting peace is deep, thorough and profound. Ideally, we would learn as we go, rather than waiting for all the hard lessons of life to hit us just before or after death....but we're not always the brightest bulbs in the pack...let's admit it. Suffering is the touchstone of spirituality....that is, until we get the message that all of life is a learning experience and it's our job to discover the lesson, not create the curriculum, we will be at the mercy of karma.

Having worked for many years on my own healing and spiritual health, and having supported numerous students, clients, patients and parishioners in doing the same, what I have come to know is that we're all in this school together....sometimes teachers, sometimes students. God, life, consciousness can use each of us to bring more love and peace into the world. When we are aware of this opportunity and sign up for it with our conscious intentions, prayer and decision to see all of our interactions from this perspective, we become part of the flow of grace that teaches us with kindness rather than comeuppance. We become instruments of grace for others as we practice forbearance, patience and trust in the justice and mercy of God's creation. We become aware of the benevolence of life even in seemingly harsh experiences like death, trauma and loss.

'It's all good' in practice looks like acceptance of what comes into and out of our lives while feeling the true experience of our heart….joy, sorrow, longing, regret, love, peace. It looks like a mindful presence that notices all the ways that Creation is trying to prove its support for us as we learn and grow. It looks like wonder, awe, gratitude. It also looks like prayerful forbearance that others would come to such a peaceful, loving and free state of being that they would no longer seek to do harm.

Once we have tasted the truth of the 'It's all good' life, we will naturally want others to experience that truth. Many will not open to it, not want it, not believe it is possible, but our desire does not go unnoticed in the realm of creation. Love begets love, and a sincere desire for good for others cannot help but get the attention of the great Source of love and life, of the angels and beings who await the chance to pour down mercy and grace upon the world to counter the great negativity that human small-mindedness has created here.

When our hearts seek to decrease the suffering of humankind and the natural world, the universe responds with wonders and miracles that astound and overwhelm our human minds. When we live by the values of kindness, compassion, love, peace, forgiveness and mercy, these weighty virtues multiply the possibilities for healing and transformation of souls and all of humankind. Each person's contribution matters in the scheme of balance between light and darkness, and we are all responsible for the state of humankind by what we put out in mind, word and action. In my experience, an act of love multiplies by the response of the universe in recognizing Itself in us. Graces and miracles follow in such powerful and awesome volume that confounds the mind and opens the heart. God magnifies our efforts and rewards us superbly and sublimely for expressing our true nature as beings of love and light.

Simple steps to 'It's all good.'

- Practice mindfulness and gratitude for your blessings.
- Look for the lesson in everything that happens to you. Everything does happen for a reason…can you see what that reason is?....or can you simply accept that the lesson is for good?
- Acknowledge, accept and validate your feelings and then move toward healing through asking for or giving forgiveness.
- Practice forgiveness and forbearance (forgiving before being apologized to), knowing that people who cause pain do so because of their own pain, not because they're bad people.
- Take responsibility for your thoughts, words and actions. Apologize when you do something unkind and sincerely ask for forgiveness. Once you've done this, watch for the miracle….even if the person you're asking won't say they forgive you, you have started the wheels in motion for grace to flow.
- Pray for yourself and for others….not that they would do what you want, but that they would feel so loved that they would be free to give and receive the love that makes life worth living.
- Pray for the world, for peace and the end to suffering….God is listening and waiting for us to do our part in pouring mercy and grace on the world to overcome the karmic debt that humankind has created. Prayer is an investment with massive returns for both the person praying and those prayed for.

- Pray for the planet and do your part in keeping her healthy, clean and adored. Our Mother Earth needs caring and loving children to restore her to health for the sake of future generations and all of humankind.

Knowing

Some truths are deeply seated and unalterable
Standing the test of time, fate and the movement of the stars
Under all that seems real but is illusion
This solid force remains unchanged
We lose ourselves to it taking on flesh
And are restored to it in awakening to life
Wisdom informing this body/mind
At once mundane and sublime
Natural reminders surround us, poking at our drowsy spirits
Sights and smells and feelings and touch
Deepened to ecstasy when seen from eternity
This world is a stage
Some sleepwalk, some awaken to play their part
In love and amusement, allowing the play to unfold
Merrily, merrily and with open heart
Taking in the joy with the sorrow, the ebb with the flow
The waxing with the waning, the union with the waiting
Urgency dissolves in presence
Peace pervades the parade
Simplicity allows for free flowing movement
Sweetness drips from the I
Sweetness and light

Heart of Gold

Sometimes I think in lyrics....

When my children were young and they would do unkind or inconsiderate things, I would admonish them to 'get their hearts on straight'. I know without a doubt that the heart of hearts in each soul created by God is a heart of gold. Under the pain, the wounding, the errors and misgivings, the fear and angst, there is a simple, beautiful creation...the human heart made by love, of love, for love. This heart of gold is not tarnished or dented by the stuff of life that is painful, hurtful or damaging. Beneath all pain this heart shines, awaiting a crack in the defensive walls built up around it in order to shine the light of love into our being, and beyond our being to others.

So how do we access this shining light within us? How do we tear down the protective barriers and live with our hearts ablaze and soft. This unveiling can feel very intimate and vulnerable...like showing the soft underbelly where those who would strike at us have an opportunity to make a direct hit with unkindness, criticism, judgment, or meanness. In reality, holding fast to the truth of our soft, strong hearts is in itself a protection. When God sees us so trusting, so open to love, He cannot help but swoop in with graceful protections that keep us safe. Our innocence restored, we are cherubim in His sight and He would do anything to keep us safe and free. Like a good father and mother, our divine parent wants nothing more for us than the full expression of our true, joyful and authentic nature…our heart of gold. What parent would not relish the sweetness of seeing a child so free? so loving and lovely? so joyful and kind? fully themselves and fully alive.

This soft, sweet innocence must not be confused with naivete, with being gullible. In fact, the more loving kindness and compassion we exude, the more powerful the force of grace surrounding us. From this invulnerable vulnerability, we can move mountains, heal hearts, and change the world. The depth of faith, trust and acceptance required to do this is nothing short of heroic. We are taught quite young to compare, compete and watch out for ourselves. We have forgotten the great truth that life watches out for us, love protects us, and innocence reveals truth in us. This truth that sets us free is a powerful energy that encompasses our being, offering strength and clarity, and a peace which passes understanding…that peace which Jesus promised us when we become like little children.

Like children, our authentic hearts are simple, pure and 'good'. I hesitate to use the word 'good' because it has been used to abuse and shame people for so long. If we were simply to remember that we were made good, made from goodness, from God, then we could let each other be. Then we wouldn't have to twist and turn ourselves in order to get attention, affection and love.

We would just know, and in that knowing we would not need to be called 'good'.

Human hearts are made to love. They are super-sensitive instruments that feel what others feel and move toward pain and sorrow with compassion; move toward love with joy. Hearts would simply speak to one another without guile, without disguise, without trying to make an impression. The beauty and purity of Mother Mary is often described in this way...the nurturing, natural love of the Great Mother who has one desire, to love us into health and wholeness. Her sweet graces bless us whenever we turn to her. Her sublime presence comforts and convinces; convinces us that we are loveable and loved.

These two things we can give one another following the Blessed Mother's example.....the acceptance and celebration of one another's loving and loveable nature. Each of us are unique and beautiful creations that share this sweet heart of gold which desires nothing more than loving connection with others, as sisters and brothers in Christ, in Love, in God, in Life.

Finding the heart of gold in yourself and others:

1.   Turn your attention inward to the center of your chest, the center of your being, and feel yourself. Seek your good heart and come to know its truth and innocence, its beauty. Spend a lot of time just feeling how loving and loveable you are.

2.   If you have trouble finding your good heart....usually due to fear that you'll find something else if you go inside there...make a simple prayer that God show you how God sees you, how God made you. Sitting in the presence of God's view of our perfectly loveable being is so healing and liberating.

3.   Once you have found your heart of gold, you can turn and seek that same heart in others. We each have a different hue, a different tone or melody, but the motivating and inspiring force is the same...love in its many expressions.

4.   Practice loving-kindness toward yourself and others when you/they forget that this ultimate truth is true about each of us....eternally and unalterably true. We can dress up as something else besides beings of love, but we will never fool our true selves or God with this masquerade. Loving-kindness and acceptance is like water and sunshine on the feeble flower of the heart. It will foster abundant blossoming and make for a most enjoyable experience in this Garden of Eden we call earth life.

hard heart

the pains our hearts endure
with battle scars twisting scar tissue
until no love can enter in
minute spaces imprisoned in iron shackles
of fear and loneliness

how shall we pry open this hard heart
resuscitate it and peel away the thick, leather straps
that block the natural and dynamic flow
barbed and spitting warnings to steer clear
angsty, impotent, indiscriminate jabs

all guards are up, shields raised
as if love were a threat to health, to peace
when lack of love is a living hell disguised as calm
set one spark near that dry tinder
and the flames of Hades spring forth

self-preservation is a farse
one cannot be preserved from life
it moves of its own accord and has its way
no matter our rebellion or seeming protection
surrender is the only choice
control is futile and bogus

and oh when gloves are off and guard is down
the sweet torment of love takes hold
a torrent of movement and grace
unmasking all parts, returned to nakedness
vulnerable, tender, afraid are we....of what
of being who we were meant to be

oh sore, soft heart that chooses life
stay open and take the jabs of the fearful
only love prevails in the end
after all the tears and heartache subside
peace, hope, joy remain to encourage and revive

The Mystery of Mysticism

'I don't want to reason anymore about the one I love, the one I love. I don't want to reason anymore about God above, God above. I just want to melt away in all its grace, drift away to that sacred place where there's no more you and me, no more they and we, just unity.'

~Trevor Hall

The ancient mysteries were well guarded and rightly so as they are powerful realities that, in the hands of darkness, could be used for evil purposes. Like the 'Law of Attraction' when bereft of selfless love becomes just about getting what the ego wants; the realities of the energetic universe reflect powers that can be used for good or evil.

I am not a fan of the word 'evil' as it has been used in religion, but if we consider 'evil' to be anything that is separate from love/connection and interested in self-promotion, power, greed and indulgence, then it is clear that the mystical laws of the universe could be usurped for unloving purposes. It is a blight on the heart of humanity when this happens...but it is also the reason we are here in this world, to choose love.

A mystic, by definition, is someone who actually, personally, intimately experiences the laws of creation in their life. Someone who is attuned to the energy of life, by practice or by grace, and who is aligned with love of God and neighbor. A mystic 'believes in the spiritual apprehension of truth beyond intellect.' One who trusts their heart of hearts, and their experiences, above their thinking mind. One who lives from the inside out rather than the outside in.

All humans have mystical experiences, sometimes called 'peak experiences' in the realm of psychology, in which they know something but don't know how/why they know it...in which they are 'guided' by an internal compass that doesn't seem to have any rhyme or reason to support it. If we were to harvest these experiences and store them up in our hearts, this gathering of treasure would shine like gold within us as a constant reminder of the deeper spiritual truth and the source of our being; wisdom.

A mystic is one who trusts this wisdom above the cogitations of the thinking mind. In our human history which has embraced, '*I think therefore I am.*' we have become far removed from this inner and innate wisdom which we share with all of creation. The Godseed of creation, of love, is deposited in all of creation, expressed in myriad forms which we are given as gifts of remembrance and joy. A tree, a flower, a river, a cloud, a fox, a child.....all begotten from that same primordial seed which is light and life and love. We see it growing, blossoming, shedding, cycling again and again; day follows night and night follows day, seasons change, humans age, meadows turn to forests, water rises and falls. All of nature is imbued with the recycling spirit that transforms but stays the same, eternal and infinite but also clear and present.

We go to nature for these experiences because nature does not resist life. As thinking beings, we have the choice to follow our intuitive nature or to talk ourselves out of it. When we are constantly distracted by materialism and consumption, we cannot hear that still small voice that is ever present in our being. When we believe we are what we think, what we emote, we lose consciousness of our being, the ground of being that the saints and sages of all ages refer us back to for our salvation and abundant life. Spiritual practices in all traditions were originally meant to restore us to connection with the inner divine, with our ground of being, our original face. As these practices became formalized and institutionalized, some used power and fear to manipulate and control those who were disconnected rather than to support their reconnection/recollection in the spirit.

Nature has being but not thought. It has expression, but not cogitation; it has truth, but not rationalization. Peeling away the layers of mind created by *civility* and sold to us as *truth* is the work of the mystics of all times. When one turns their life in this direction, others often pooh-pooh them; judge, criticize, lower their opinion of the truth-seeker.

As an educated woman, a religious woman, a spiritual woman, I have been on the receiving end of much criticism, judgment and character assassination. In the earthly life, it is painful and challenging to keep one's heart open to love and the movement of the spirit when attacks are waged from all sides to diminish and defame. And yet, the spirit's voice, once freed, will not let us be. It will not be drowned out by the raging masses of rational minds that cannot see or hear their own truths.

Jesus said those who seek truth, who seek God, will be persecuted. The masses of people do not want to be awoken and, like an irritated and groggy person who flails aggressively at the alarm clock on their nightstand, most people do not awaken gracefully. I did not awaken gracefully. Growing pains, acting out, crushing delicate flowers underfoot, I was raised up to the sublime by the gradual understanding of truth which humbles us and fosters compassion in our hearts for those who follow. Who can judge the awakening of others when our own was so graceless.

And then again, as the spirit awakens, gratitude swells in our heart for the sometimes painful, sometimes ecstatic process of awakening. With more and more convincing experience, the mystic chooses a life driven by inner urgings over a life reactive to outer stimuli. And this sweet life proves itself over and over, it multiplies love in us until we overflow with this truth and, in the eyes of the world, this peace which passes understanding can look like madness, disconnection or lack of concern. In fact, it is a constant remembering that the experiences of the mind-life are painful, repetitive and false, whereas those of the spirit are life-enhancing, deepening, transformative and universally true.

So, who do we follow? Which saints, sages, pro~~fits~~ phets, saviors of the soul? Which practices, religions, philosophies, ideas, urgings? If God is an ocean of Universal Love, what matter is it the stream we take to return to it? Division and comparison of any sort is a mind-made monster. Unity and oneness in the many draws us back to our Self, the one Self; that ocean and that love, that cycle of incarnation and reunion. Let's not continue to be distracted by the different routes we take to return to love. Let others be on their way and you be on yours. The unique but universal truth will draw each of us home. In this we can trust. In this way we can follow those who speak to our spirit and be followed by those who hear our heartsong and are moved by it. What a pleasant route to return….friends in either direction….teachers and students and lovers and friends. What a happy journey we are on….when we listen and remember.

I Am That

I Am That, the sweet, good wave of love and life
I Am That, the depth that has no end and no beginning
Not separate from life, from movement, from illusion
But maker of the dream in mind which tangles and hides
Come out, wherever you are,
Come out and in, into the deep place where peace lives
Where you dwell, and where you sprang from
You are returning without leaving
Reuniting without dividing, without separating
How strange and true this trick of Self
Awakening to the game as the Game Master
How subtle the view from here, filmy shadows
No weight or sound, phantasms that convince, delude
Search no more, you are That too
Victory over the world, over time
Eternity is here
Praise be to Christ, the great I AM.

Disciplines vs. Practices

'You are the air I breathe. Your holy spirit living in me. And I am lost without you. And I am desperate for you.'

~*Michael W. Smith*

A seeker starts down a path to reunion by making spiritual disciplines into spiritual practices. Like any new habit or pattern, one must be somewhat seriously dedicated to performing a particular task repeatedly until it becomes part of our being and we see the deeper, subtler results arise. This is the part of the journey where one is focused on 'disciplines'. Disciplines turn us into disciples, followers of truth.

In nearly all spiritual traditions, there are practices like meditation, prayer, chanting, service and study that support a return to Self and a reunion with Creation. These 'yogas' extract us from the mind of the world and restore us to the Mind of Creation, the Mind of God, the Christ-Mind, Buddha-Mind, Brahma-Mind. Before they become practices, or patterns in our life/being, they are disciplines.....things we make ourselves do until they are so much a part of us that we do them without effort. Once our habitual being is on board with the result of the disciplines, they become practices which maintain our connection with Self and Truth in a world full of distractions and temptations which would pull us away from this inner knowing and peace.

Sometimes people have spiritual or religious 'baggage'....wounds caused by the unforgiving strictness and guilt-producing stigma of a religious, spiritual or philosophical institution. This baggage makes them reticent to continue with a particular set of practices as they dredge up negative experiences and feelings from their history. It is understandable that we would want to avoid those things which brought us pain. We are creatures of habit, after all. In psychology, Carl Rogers says that the *fully functioning person* is one who can move in any direction at any time.....this would look like a person who could engage in his/her historical religious/spiritual practice having healed themselves of the damage done by it. This is a high calling and most will avoid returning to the scene of those spiritual crimes in favor of another flavor, another stream or path to return to love.

Whatever you choose, whichever tradition or teacher, you will need to choose it truly and deeply in order to dive into the subtleties of the tradition and reap the benefits of it. One could float along the surface of a particular practice, feeling good and considering that they're gaining all that is to be gained from that tradition. In reality, it is the diving deeply that gets us to the nuggets of real gold that rest on the riverbed. The glittering sunshine on the surface can distract us for a long time before we become aware that there is a depth beneath us that we have not plumbed.

This superficial experience, though pleasant, is but a feather on the surface of the water which does not know that there are depths beneath it which will dismantle the ego and transform the being. In these eclectic and 'new age' times, many people get distracted by the experience of the feather....light, flowing on the stream, effortless and lovely. This is where the discipline is needed....and why the teacher/guru traditions arose. The guide that tugs at the complacent feather, pulling it underwater to anchor it firmly in the riverbed to be nourished by the true gold. Feathers don't always enjoy this process. It requires discipline and obedience to truth over ego....but even that is a process, letting go of an attachment to who we think we are in order to find out who we are in truth.

Obedience is a dirty word in our culture but it really means 'to listen'. Listening to one who has been further along the path or deeper into the tradition will aide us on our journey to full consciousness. If we cannot listen, we cannot learn. If we will not listen, we will not grow. The teacher is one who restores us to our true Self. The teacher does not create our true Self, does not discover it, but points us firmly in its direction until we reach it, embrace it and become inextricable from it. Then the teacher becomes our friend, our companion in the joy of the awakened life.

Conversely, I see some who strive for discipline in such an urgent and intense way that they miss the sweetness of the journey, as if the discipline were the reward. These folks feel they must prove themselves to God, to life, by working hard and never letting up. Although self-discipline and intentional, consistent practices do help us to anchor in truth, if we are so militant about the practices, we will miss the joys and graces that make the process of transformation a love affair between consciousness and Self; between the soul and God. How sad to reach the finish line to find the spoils overlooked in our intense focus on finishing.

The Buddha points us to the middle way. Jesus says to come to him as a little child to receive the kingdom. Our egos need discipline only until they fall in love, at which time they are transformed into servants of the inner truth that is our Self, and supporters of the intimate and ecstatic union of Soul and Self which is the divine romance and the blissful reward for returning to Love.

So, discipline the body/mind/ego/emotions until they get on board and have steady practices that keep the flow of Love open in the heart. The sweet innocence of true love will do the rest. Then the whole river will be imbued with the golden hue of truth that will carry us in grace and ground us in the magnificent power of Creation. Then we will at last be reunited to the Love from whence we came. Love restored has a sweetness that is the golden nectar of the mystic. Such sweetness overshadows all earthly beauty but also enlivens it as we see each wonder of creation as an expression of God's deep and abiding love for us, gifts from the Giver of Life for our soul's journey. This kind of aliveness creates the peace which passes understanding, the abundant life, the nirvana, the samadhi, the heaven on earth that seekers seek.

The Eucharist

Holy Sacrament that restores me to Life
Daily bread infused with Grace
I call upon my Lord to move heaven and earth
To make the elixir that erases sin

He moves and makes His Presence known
A bolt of Love, a breeze of peace
The air rarified as I intone
The command that brings His blessed hand

Like lightening to a lightening rod
The force of will and devotion
Draws down His precious gift
Given to me, and through me, to them

Whoever wants His grace receives
Through hands and feet made right by Him
The blessed feast which knows no end
Blood and body in this servant's hands.

And oh, what crazy joy to serve
The feast of feasts that rescues souls
From darkness' clutch and Satan's bands
That tie the soul to sin and dust

Oh, make us new, my Holy Prince,
Make us ever more like you
Transfixed by Love and saved by Grace
We walk the earth to do your will.

Light unceasing and increasing
Ecstatic union with the Most High
Flesh made new and heart made pure
The Sacred Mystery shines from our eyes.

Many Paths

'There's many roads and many paths that lead to you. Some say they're false but I believe all of them are true, the green earth and the sky blue. Yes and baby, baby, I'm a fool, a fool without you...a fool without you.'

~Trevor Hall

Having studied everything from Native American Spirituality to Christian Mysticism, from Theravada Buddhism to Kundalini Yoga, and many traditions and practices in between, I have come full circle from my younger self who was driven by the question of why peoples who say they love God are at odds with one another. I was driven to find the common denominator in all traditions and, over 30 years, many disciplines and practices, life experiences and lessons, I come to sit squarely at the meeting point of all traditions, the center of the four directions, the four noble truths, the four archangels....where all are pointing the way home to the center and ground of being, though following different paths.

Why are we humans so small minded as to think that God can be boxed into our earthly ideas? The many faces and expressions of God are miraculous and beautiful, terrifying and awesome. A newborn child formed in a woman from the union of 2 cells. A tornado that ravages the earth with its tunnel of wind. The delicate spider web. The gruesomeness of the spider's prey caught in a trap and cocooned alive to await its captor's bloodlust.

A God to be feared and loved, an awesome God who wields the power to create, mitigate and destroy. This trinity appears in all traditions....creator, destroyer, sustainer; creator, mediator, holy spirit; love, justice, grace; the three faces of God that describe the fascinating and wondrous creation and cycles of life, death and rebirth.

I am an intense person. When my heart or soul longs for something, resistance if futile, like trying to hold back the tide. I have not perfected the art of obedience to the still small voice, the 'listening' and 'following without question' that all of my teachers have recommended. I am impatient, impudent, rebellious and wild, as God painted me. I am also sensitive, vulnerable, loyal and deep. My heart has lived with this inner paradox alternately hating one or the other of these parallel and sometimes converging qualities of this particular incarnation. I am an enigma even to myself; especially to myself. I am the irreverent Reverend Mary Francis. I sing God's praises and I swear like a trooper. I dance in spiritual ecstacy with the kirtan of voice and spirit, I enjoy the physical ecstacy of a lover's embrace. These paradoxes are confounding but also relaxing. My life has been a crooked journey which to many in the mainstream world-mind seems eccentric at best and blasphemous at worst. I am as the joker or the trickster; sage and wild, causing contradictions that defy reason and restore sight. This has been my path....lover of life, lover of God, lover of the light, fierce advocate for truth, tender friend of the downtrodden, guide for the seeker.

Whatever path you choose, or are chosen by, do not fear the throngs who will berate, negate and attempt to diminish your heartsong. They do not know what you are called to. Do not allow their stifling rationalism and grandiose criticisms to weigh down your spirit. They are busy comparing while you are busy living. They are busy condemning while you are busy loving. Let go the hold they have on you and your sense of worth, your truth. Bless them and send them on their way, and take your own way, alone if you must. The solitary way is only solitary until you encounter the great Lover upon your own heart's path and are embraced in the all-encompassing and ecstatic love of complete acceptance, mutual adoration, gratitude and grace that arises from the soul's encounter with Self, with God.

But neither be shallow and easily sated by the illusory pleasantries of the lower spiritual realms. Like phantoms stuck to the earth for fear of losing its pleasures, spirits can be distracted by the glitter of the first few experiences of energy, light, love and peace that are given as gifts in reserve for the real and dangerous work of overcoming the ego without inflating it further. If you step only a few steps in, you will become a spiritual achiever who wears those first shiny experiences like a badge of honor, self-proclaimed. If you continue, you will be annihilated and dispossessed of the illusion that you are *all that*. In this ego annihilation is your freedom and your truth. When there is nothing left to be, then you can just be. This cosmic riddle only makes sense from the other side of it. We spend hours and days and years trying to 'be' somebody, rather than just being. In this beingness we are simple and kind, wise and loving; true to our nature as beings of light and love. The mind, body, ego, emotions, all take their rightful place as the vehicle of expression for the spirit.

This is where the fun begins....you and God expressing through the unique form that was created as your masterpiece. How delightful and diverse this instrument can be when moved by spirit. How surprisingly light and deep, harsh and holy. The paradox continues expressed in and through you as Boddhisatva...to shatter the illusions that others live under and compassionately love them into wakefulness.

Does your mind know the *right* path to take? the *right* field to lie in? No, but your heart and your spirit when allowed will show you the way without fail. You will not falter when others put stumbling blocks before you. You will not be waylaid or distracted. You will not know why you must go where you must go, but you will go anyway. Find your heart, trust your heart, obey your heart until it lands you squarely at the center of the circle, the cell of life that is God's seed in you. Then you will make your way back into the world, transformed and transfigured by the love of the Great Lover.

Whose house is this?

This is my house
I will choose the furniture and curtains
I will paint the walls as I choose
I will leave it clean or messy

I am not in need of guidance
My choices teach me all I need to know
What brings peace, I will repeat
What brings turmoil, I will reject

I am the master of this house
It does not need a manager or doctor
It needs my attentive care and love
To choose what suits me truly

Is there another who can answer
What is the best choice for me
For the house in which I live and rest
The sanctuary of my heart and soul

No.....it is I alone who choose
I alone who decide such things
Guided by history and honest friends
Spurred on by hope and a desire to grow

My capacious heart will be my guide
I will protect its right to choose
I will keep it open in spite of dangers
I will fill my house with song

And those who hear my music will dance along
In my house....the one I build....the one I love
And there will be rejoicing and praise
For all that is good within and without

And peace will reign there
Peace and joy and gratitude
In this house of mine
In this heart of mine

Suffering and Sacrifice

We only have to suffer until we learn to accept.
We only have to sacrifice until we learn to love.

Suffering and sacrifice are two areas of spirituality that most people would like to flee from. They are seen as outdated notions in the new age realm of 'spirit as love'. On the surface this is true. In essence, we do not need to prove ourselves to God in order to be loved, we are loved by the nature of being created by God. We can enjoy the beauties of life in all its richness and splendor. The Buddhists would admonish us that all suffering comes from attachment, so if we simply practice nonattachment, we will no longer suffer. Modern thinkers disdain the sacrifice that Christ made for humankind as inhumane and gruesome rather than heroic and loving. We don't like discomfort so we rationalize away suffering and sacrifice, or we wear it like self-flagellation that is as prideful as self-adulation.

Once again, I direct you toward the depth of any spiritual teaching which goes beyond the milk and honey given to spiritual infants to coax their growth and sweeten their way. When we begin a spiritual path, God understands that we need coaxing and coddling, like a young child, to grow in the ways of righteousness and truth. We feed our children soft foods, hold their hand as they learn to walk, soothe their fevers and calm their fears. And then comes a point in maturity where the parent becomes the teacher, still loving and kind, but also fair and firm in teaching the truths of life. Kindness, compassion, generosity, selflessness are taught by example and admonition, if a parent is really parenting.

When my children were unkind to someone, I would gently remind them to do unto others as they would have done unto them. This golden rule is part of every tradition and religion, every philosophy and belief system. Love begets love. But sometimes children are selfish, mean-spirited and hurtful. Sometimes they cause suffering or harm, break things or speak disrespectfully. Parents are meant to remedy these errors with kind but firm teachings to help raise up the child into a fine young adult who expresses the goodness inherent to their nature.

Spiritual teachers do the same. When we are 'suffering' they redirect our thinking and teach us to go to God/Love for comfort and strength without turning spiteful. They teach us it is better to give than to receive, that sacrificing on behalf of someone who has less brings untold blessings and espouses kindness in the receiver. Love begets love.

On the highest level of spirit, all suffering is seen as purposeful, though maybe sorrowful; all sacrifice is seen as mature love which suffers so others need not suffer. Many saints and sages suffered for humankind in an effort to free the sleepwalking from the consequence of their unconscious actions. Jesus 'took on the sins of the world', and suffered the karma of earthly sin in order to free us to reunite with God. If any of us did not have the help of these spiritual beings who are heroes of love, we would be floundering in the karmic cycle into eternity. It is with gratitude and love that I acknowledge Jesus, Buddha, Mohammed, Abraham, and all other beings who have gone before, paving the way to atonement by taking on the karmic debt of humankind. Jesus said, 'Forgive them, Father, they know not what they do.' This kind of sacrifice is almost unheard of these days, even scoffed at. And yet, this high spiritual attribute is not just suffering for the sake of suffering, for a martyrdom that yields no grace. It is bearing one another's burden by choosing to carry it with them. It is showing up with a heart that will love in the face of pain, in the face of meanness, and taking one for the team so that one soul might be freed from that karmic cycle.

Like Gandhi's salt flat brigade who allowed themselves to be beaten by the British soldiers until the soldiers lost the will to beat them, falling on their knees in surrender and humility, we can learn to 'turn the other cheek', 'love our enemies', 'give our shirt along with our coat'. We can learn to suffer and sacrifice in this way, but not until we have been thoroughly convinced of the love that created and sustains us. This love must be secured into our bones and being, having healed all former wounds and afflictions, we are convicted by the faithful, trusting knowing that our efforts will alleviate the felt suffering of others and we do not mind being instruments of suffering and sacrifice if it will bring peace to our brothers and sisters. Suffering and sacrifice without retaliation and without self-adulation. In reality this is love; a high love that few understand or emulate, but love nonetheless.

My brother's keeper

How do you entrust my brother to me? my sister?
You have seen my imperfections and trials
You know my hard-hearted and hard-headed ways
And yet you place before me one more wounded than I
More broken and destitute
And you ask my assistance

Counting my blessings and pulling on bootstraps
I turn with compassionate heart
To ease the suffering I see
Though I know not how it is done
A simple desire, a simple presence, a simple prayer
I offer myself as an instrument of whatever grace may flow through me
Not by my merit but by your mercy

And I am in awe, in wonder of the wonders that occur

As one heart feels seen and received by another

As one soul's thirst is quenched by love

I offer my heart for such purposes

Though I know not from where the strength will come

From where the words will come

I offer myself, blind and dumb, weak and weary

To be a water-bearer for the parched souls of the dying, the lonely, the desperate

I offer my unworthy heart, my selfish heart

That your blessing might bless me as it passes to my brother

That I also might be healed and made whole in your sight, by your sight

And some miracle of relief occurs, though no circumstance has changed

Love has been communicated, received and returned

Both restored by its eternal truth

Enlightenment & Self-Realization

'Chop that wood, carry water. What's the sound of one hand clapping? Enlightenment, don't know what it is.' ~Van Morrison

Since Buddhism came into vogue in the west, enlightenment has been seen as a goal of the spiritual life. Enlightenment, or illumination as it is called in Christianity, is the state of being lighted from within. The 'Age of Enlightenment' was a time when humans put reason above experience, superstition and tradition; a much-needed break from patterns of mindless thought, belief and behavior, but also a thorn in the side of the mystic whose true, spiritual experiences and visions would be relegated to insanity or wishful thinking. We have gone so far as to use the study of brain activity to imply that our brain has a 'belief in God' section, as it has a section for sight and smell. Interestingly, this theory, as many scientific observations do, only reports on an observation of brain activity, it does not make a direct causal relationship between the brain activity and what instigated it. This is the small mind trying to explain away the great mind simply because it is beyond reason. Enlightenment is the state of being guided by inner light, the inner divine, the inner knower, who is the spouse of the soul and the emanation of God; light, life and love.

Jesus's transfiguration, or illumination, is described in the Bible as His body being filled with light, and emanating light from His center which transformed and transfigured His being into the full expression of Man-God, of Christ. Jesus was christed, filled with the light of Christ which is the essence of God and the expression of love and wisdom. He fully manifested this as a spirit in the material world in order to teach us, and show us by His example, how to live and how to love. He cared no longer for the things of the world but was single-minded and single-hearted on sharing the saving graces of God's mercy, forgiveness and atonement with all of us.

Jesus was 'Self-Realized', or 'God-Realized', the full incarnation of the Light of Christ. Each of us strive toward incarnating spirit fully into the flesh. We are distracted by worldly things, slowed by indulgences and addictions, and waylaid by karmic consequences until we look to the giver of life for guidance and truth. When we do the disciplines and practices that extract us from material life, we turn our hearts and minds toward the spirit. Once embodied, we turn our spiritual being back toward the earth to express its truth and shine its light. Jesus reminds us that we are the *'light of the world'*.

In many esoteric and mystical traditions, there are initiations or rituals that assist the neophyte in opening to and containing the light, consciousness and reality of union with God and expression of the GodSelf. Are there souls who receive these blessings and attunements from the spirit? Certainly, that is God's prerogative. Having a teacher, priest, monk, or guide in the flesh who is living at this level of consciousness is an earthly help; a helper who can also provide the seeker with guidance and support in coming into the Light, and into Union with God; Enlightenment and Self-Realization respectively.

At each level of consciousness, a seeker will be drawn to a teacher of the caliber needed to progress to the next level of insight and expansion until the GodSelf is revealed within them as the eternal Teacher and Guide of the Soul. This is not merely intuition, but the reality of God's being in union with your very soul that becomes the guiding force for all thought, word and deed. Daily practices help us to maintain connection and consciousness of Self until we are fully integrated and remain in Self despite any distraction or contrary idea. God has fully proven Godself to us and in us. Our confidence in Self is warranted by its absolute perfection as we flow in the grace of a spirit-filled life divined for God's purposes. We become instruments of peace and love, of awakening as God moves us as willing pawns to fulfill St. Francis' prayer.

The Saint Francis Prayer:

Make me a channel of your peace
Where there is hatred, let me bring your love
Where there is sadness, ever joy
And where there's doubt, true faith in you
Oh, Master, grant that I may never seek
So much to be consoled as to console
To be understood as to understand
To be loved, as to love with all my soul
Make me a channel of your peace
It is in pardoning that we are pardoned
In giving of ourselves that we receive
And in dying that we're born to eternal life.

These sage words, this soul plea, could be the practice of a lifetime. With heartfelt desire and devotion we can pray or chant this famous, simple supplication and expect to be held and helped as we grow into its graceful beauty as a soul loving people for God.

Do not expect to be known or noticed for this. Jesus' words are true; these things are for those with *eyes to see and ears to hear*. But your sisters and brothers in Love will surround you with loving support and prayers and you will not be alone. Though solitary in your service, you will have the aide of saints and angels, in and out of the flesh, to see into you and rejoice in the realizations that have come to fruition in you.

If They Only Knew

Shall I reply in outward form when blind ones cannot see past the dark attire which absorbs the sins and sorrows of man?

Shall I shed Light once again by tearing open my chest to bear the joyful treasure that God has placed therein?

Shall I testify to the ecstasy which is God in my flesh?

What gems and treasures must I bear, that God's sweet love has given me?

Intimate gifts, sublime and pure.

What words have I this mortal mouth, this stifling mind, to spread the wings of heaven's song for those to hear who cannot hear?

My flesh afire with holy love; my heart enlarged and burning.

God's mind in every cell of my being; alive, vibrant and tantalizing me to lose myself inside the great sea of sweetness and light that sits just behind my eyes and under my skin.

If not for the sweet call of my Lord to love the people as I am loved, I would surrender to the union which nullifies me and glorifies Thee.

Do they know, can they know, will they know the supernatural beauty and bliss that I am?

I know not how my flesh retains form.

I know not how my flesh continues to obey the laws of earth.

Only by God's grace and command do I remain here.

Angels holding me fast so I do not fly away home as yet.

SECTION II:

<u>PRACTICE</u>

Relaxing into Love

We are so trained to think with an achievement mentality, that we have forgotten that it is in Love, in God, that we live and move and have our being. The sense of urgency and importance that fuels our daily activities hides the pure flowing and dynamic river of grace which sustains us in spirit and in body. How have we been so convinced that we must toil and suffer in order to be successful, to be worthy? All manner of activity and achievement can bring accolades and prestige, shoring up the ego for another day of seemingly worthwhile living, but no activity, no achievement, no proof can bring the solace our heart and soul is dying for, crying for.

It is not until we let go and relax into the reality of Love that we can become thoroughly convinced, thoroughly imbued with the great and gentle truth that we are already seen, known and loved by the source of all Life. When we turn away from external expectations and admonitions, into the depths of our being, we will find a deep well of contentment and peace in which to rest. This deep peace, this deep rest, is a convalescence for our soul which has been trying to keep up with the restless, striving mind which drives the body and heart to distraction. Turning inward restores us to ourselves, the witness behind the activity; mental, emotional and physical.

Take a look at your yesterday. Were you present to it? What invisible force was driving your activity? Duty, achievement, success, money, responsibility, fear, unworthiness? Be honest with yourself and reflect on why you do what you do, think what you think, feel what you feel. If you have done any work on healing your wounds, healing your mind/emotions/body, you will have some clarity of sight as you introspect the moments and hours and days of your life. If you are unsettled and lacking in contentment, it is likely that you have disconnected from your true source of knowing and have given over this wise power to a much smaller and less conscious part of yourself....the part that will drive you to distraction, the part that will use guilt and shame to force your hand. Only love will heal this cycle that has been usurped by the small ego mind which strives to preserve itself no matter the cost.

In essence, we can only be restored to love by surrendering all other duties and distractions. We have to let go into it....a saying which has been used superficially in many spiritual/self-help circles. Letting go is not just turning away from something you cannot change, it is turning toward something that ultimately has your back, and your heart, at all times. This something, this love, is accepting, unconditional, ever-present, convincing, soothing, strengthening, attentive, sweet, quiet, powerful.....all the support our spirits need to heal, shine and thrive. But first comes the relaxing...the hardest part and the longest journey from head to heart, from activity to stillness, from noise to silence.

Time out of mind, and Mind out of time. This is where we are going to find true peace, gentle love, quiet wisdom. Never admonishing or punishing, the love from which you sprang is a wellspring of rest and acceptance. It convinces every part of you that you are held in the gentle power of creation, the sweet lover of your soul that knows every hair on your head and watches over every breath you take. Resting often and deeply in this place allows for you to build a sense of trust and, beyond faith, a firm knowing, from your own experience, that all is well with your soul.

Spiritual and religious traditions have served to point us in the direction of this stillness and the still, small voice that abides there awaiting our return; awaiting our attention that it might guide us in love in a manner which perfectly suits our nature and our destiny. This is the place from which we learn our purpose in incarnating at this time on this planet. This is the depth from which we can touch into the great flow of wisdom that informs and transforms us; uncovering the original blueprint of our lives so that we might follow it without reservation or resistance. In this peace we relax enough to accept the love that animates our flesh and uses us as instruments of love and peace.

How do we get there? How do we rest there? How do we stay there? How do we live from there? We practice, practice, practice turning within, sitting in silence, opening to receive, marinating in the liquid light and love that permeates our being, our mind and our flesh. A sweet calm is restored, a deep peace which passes understanding. This inner knower/ knowing becomes our teacher and guide....but it is not a passive force, it is life itself enlivening and enlightening us. As we relax and let down our defenses, it is as if a dam were opened in us to allow more flow of love and grace. Gradually we open the floodgates wider and wider until we are no longer in need of the dam at all and can dismantle it as the waters of life are balanced and free flowing from spirit to form.

And then the dance. And then the song. And then our original face and our true voice surface to bless the world with the life we have come to live; the love we have come to give. And we, in love with love, open to the sublime and divine dance with other souls as we continue consciously in this field of love in which we live and move and have our being.

innocence

the simple sweetness of the heart
no complications or ruminations
that formless space that knows truth
without tethers to the world

what now, rest and love and joy
as time passes and I stand still
open to the freshness of each moment
as God delivers life to me and me to life

returning now and again and now
when forgetting clouds my sight
to the Self that is wide open
simple, discerning, wise

and what joy to share God in me
present in each moment to what arises
heat and light and cool soft breeze
passing over the full emptiness of my being

show only that and all are blessed
by that simple truth that gives us rest
in the spirit of God, of life and love
we remain as one

The Power of Prayer

The Offering

Whatever your heart needs to say to your God, say it
With few words or many, with form or not
God reads between lines and letters and in the silence
The deep desire of your heart to join with Love
Fear not that you do not know the way
God has never left you

Offer your heart and know it is heard, seen, known
Let fly the deep truths and sorrows that you hold
Let love be restored in your soul that you might walk
more lightly
Filled with the peace of Love's presence in you
Now you have been set free of fear
Restored to innocence and wonder

Prayer is talking to God. Like picking up a phone and directing it to *'Call God'* we have easy access to the strength and spirit of creation which surrounds and infuses us. Some say it is outdated and won't even use the word *prayer,* saying that they are sending thoughts or good energy rather than admitting that they are praying. Prayer is an expression of the heart's desire for goodness and blessings to come upon someone we love or have concern for. As creative beings, we have access to the great source of life and love, and our hearts and minds can wield those forces of creation as we please. Semantics aside, we are supplicating and directing the essence of life itself to offer life, love, comfort, healing, and peace to the subject of our prayer.

Then comes the question, who are we praying to? Again the painful residue of man-made religious institutions makes people shy or disdaining of praying to a *Being*. By what name should we call it? God, Allah, Abba, Rama, Source, Creation, Love? Does it matter? The source of life is not diminished by our disdain or enhanced by our reverence. It all boils down to the relationship you have with the forces of creation, with the energy of life, with the essence of love.

The only one who loses when we resist using one of God's names is us; the human, the fleshly being who could access all the sweet power of the universe by acknowledging it. We have been so disillusioned by the human creation of religion and ritual that we tend to throw the baby out with the bathwater; the love out with the liturgy.

God is not offended or dismissed by this. The Creator, Source of Life, Light and Love, is not diminished in any way by our philosophical tantrums and platitudes. Call It what you like, but not out of rebellion and pride. Call It out of devotion, reverence and respect; call It out of love. Then It cannot resist to distribute its power and healing at your request, at your command.

When we surrender into the Great Love relationship with the Creator, the love affair is so intense and delicate, so sweet and sublime, that all human understanding and philosophy fades into meaninglessness. So, first things first, go inside and find the source of Love and let yourself be loved until you are so in love with Love that you cannot breath or move without feeling its life-giving presence, its sweet ecstasy. Then your prayer will be a whisper into your Lover's ear, and it will be God's great pleasure to give you what you want, what you desire and ask for in the pureness of your being and in the goodness of your spirit.

In humility, we must know that as humans we are not privy to all of the workings of the mind of God all of the time. As such, we should remember in prayer that God has a plan for every being and God knows best how to work that plan through. God wants to hear our concerns and desires for our lives and the lives of others, for the planet, but God also knows what is best and, as a good, just and wise parent, will not always grant us our every desire. In the end we will see how all things work for good in God. In the moments of stress and strain, in the challenges of life, we may not always see that clearly.

So.....patience, my friends. Speak the true and deep desires of your heart to your Creator, then let them go with the wise knowing that Life has a course of its own to take. We sometimes can have an influence on that with our love and desire, and sometimes not. That part is not our call. It is wise counsel to allow the Great Source of Creation to have the final call in such matters. It is wise and humble to prostrate our tiny humanness to the beings who have gone before us and lived and learned to love in power and purity. We can pray to the saints, to the angels, to the Blessed Mother, to Jesus the Christ, to Buddha, Muhammed, Abraham, Krishna.....to all who have come before and who continue to bless us from the other side of life with their wisdom, protection and love.

If we are all one with God, it does not diminish God for us to pray to God's created beings who are reunited with love. There are so many spiritual beings available to help us. Why be rebellious and juvenile in disregarding the help that is at your beck and call? Why be irreverent and discourteous to those who are the Masters of Love. We are small creatures in comparison...let's not forget this as we grow in consciousness through the spiritual adolescence that makes us behave disrespectfully toward those who deserve our honor and respect. Our spiritual elders understand our lack of development, but how embarrassing it is to the spirit to become aware of our cheeky insolence toward these great ones who await our call for help. Just accept that there are beings, both in the flesh and beyond the flesh, who have powers that you have not yet mastered, and wisdom that you have not yet gained. Seek their wise counsel and support with reverence and respect and you will have their powerful assistance and graces in all that you do and all that you desire.

There are many, many prayers that serve us well, from many traditions. The following are prayers that I have learned by heart and use frequently, along with the St Francis prayer given earlier. These are very powerful prayers to be spoken with deep understanding, reflection, reverence and supplication. For too long, these prayers have become rote religious responsibilities and those praying have been disconnected from the great power they avail us. Spontaneous prayer from the heart is God's delight, and these prayers are our aides passed down through the ages by those who have gone before us. I use both in my prayer life, along with the unceasing prayer; the silent, prayerful emanation of love and desire for peace which streams from my heart to God's heart on behalf of humankind and the earth. Find what works for you. Do not dismiss, degrade or diminish what works for others. Add your heartfelt prayers to the supplications reaching up to heaven, to Life, for the consciousness of humanity to be restored to love.

The Lord's Prayer

Our Father who art in heaven, hallowed be Thy name

Thy kingdom come, Thy will be done

On earth as it is in heaven.

Give us this day our daily bread

And forgive us our debts (trespasses) as we forgive our debtors (those who trespass against us)

And lead us not into temptation,

But deliver us from evil

For Thine is the kingdom, and the power and the glory forever.

Amen.

The 23rd Psalm

God is my shepherd, I shall not want

He makes me to lie down in green pastures

He leads me beside the still waters

He restores my soul

He leads me in the paths of righteousness for His namesake

Yeah, though I walk through the valley of the shadow of death, I shall fear no evil

For Thou art with me

Thy rod and Thy staff they comfort me

Thou preparest a table before me in the presence of mine enemies

Though annointest my head with oil

My cup runneth over

Surely goodness and mercy shall follow me

All the days of my life

And I shall dwell in the house of my God forever

Amen.

The Rosary/The Hail Mary

Hail Mary, Full of Grace

The Lord is with Thee

Blessed art Thou among women

And blessed is the fruit of your womb, Jesus

Holy Mary, Mother of God

Pray for us sinners, now and at the hour of our death.

Amen.

The Chaplet of Divine Mercy

Oh, Glorious Father, I offer the body and blood, soul and divinity, of your dearly beloved son, our Lord, Jesus Christ, in atonement for our sins and those of the whole world.

For the sake of His sorrowful passion, have mercy on us, and on the whole world.

The 99 Names of Allah
The Japji Sahib
Kirtan Chants

Unburdening the Spirit

I have worked with Hospice patients for nearly a decade now, plus a decade of ministry and nearly 30 years of teaching and counseling. People's spirits are burdened, heavy-laiden with scars, secrets, regrets and pain. People have generally been convinced that they are neither lovable nor loved. People have twisted and turned themselves in an effort to gather crumbs of life-giving attention and affection that the spirit needs in order to survive, much less to thrive.

I remember hearing about those orphanages in eastern Europe where infants who were fed and cared for physically were dying of a mysterious syndrome called 'failure to thrive.' The human body will not sustain itself when there is no love or hope for love. Having been raised by generation after generation of oppressed, imprisoned, tortured, abused people, the human race seems to have forgotten how to support the natural, wondrous thriving of a child's spirit, or to restore a broken-spirited adult to a healthy spiritual balance.

We must unburden our souls by reflecting on our own lives, our own wounds, our own stories. We must acknowledge the good, the bad and the ugly for what it is, and what it was. We must validate our own experience with empathy and compassion so that we no longer need to strive for validation from others. We need to forgive and release ourselves and others for the hurtful, unconscious and malicious thoughts, words and deeds we have inflicted on one another.

Forgiveness is another of those precepts that is often dismissed as spiritual/religious/old-school/mumbo-jumbo. People feel self-righteous in being angry at those who have harmed them, and retaliatory in hating the hater. How is it that we are so slow to understand that two wrongs don't make a right? Haven't our mothers taught us this age-old truism? Do we listen at all to our mothers, to our ancestors, to the great teachers and sages who have come before us? Or are we so arrogant as to think that we can make our way just fine without such wisdom? Our culture in general is terribly adolescent in its approach to life. We are materialists, individualists, and consumers who indulge our every urge and whim, look out for number one, and think that the one with the most toys before death is the winner.

These delusions burden us deeply. As our outer, ego-self gathers the spoils of a self-serving life, the heart and soul of us is mortified nearly unto death. When I sit at the deathbed of a patient, they do not tell me how much money they earned or how many things they acquired, they wrestle with what their lives meant, how they contributed to life in their family, community and world. They tell me about the values they have instilled in their children; values of honesty, integrity, hard work and kindness. They do not tell me of their victories over their enemies, they tell me sadly of lost love and the futility of fighting.

In the Buddhist tradition, we are taught to 'practice death.' To remember in each moment that we are living; to be fully alive and present to life. To have our hearts open and on-line for the experiences of life, whether we judge them as joyful or sorrowful. Forgiveness of the past, compassion and forbearance for the unconsciousness of humans, and mindfulness of the present moment are what relieve the spirit and unburden the heart. This deep understanding allows for an inner freedom that is accepting and kind, alive and thriving. It is not a simple-minded attitude, rather a state of being procured by intense concentration on truth.

Once again, all traditions, religions, philosophies and spiritualities worth their mettle advise these practices and precepts be espoused and cultivated. Our efforts are repaid by an ease of acceptance, compassion and empathy for the suffering of others, and a spirit unburdened of pain and resentment. We free others and ourselves in forgiveness and compassion and open our hearts to love gently and freely no matter the circumstance or life condition we find ourselves in.

Open Heart

*Remain open, heart of mine, regardless of the weather
outside or inside. Remain soft and malleable to love, no
tethers holding one fast, no anchors slowing the flow.
Remember, oh heart, the hardened days, when nothing
moved beyond the gate that held us fast. Remember and
stay open to the simple beauty of love and life moving
through and having its way. Sometimes gentle other
times thrashing, life's movement and seasons continue.
Where will we go from here, no way of knowing....only
trusting in love's goodness. Stay open, heart of mine,
for the joys and sorrows that lie ahead. Stay open and
let it have its way with you, the threshing floor that hulls
the stalk, revealing life-giving grain, ground to nourish
more hearts. Tears and blood, heat and light pour in to
make the holy bread that saves. Make it in me, oh heart
of gold, that human kind may find its rest and take in
love. Oh then the sweetness will arise, in joy and light
as new life enters, restored to that inner celestial home
with rejoicing and peace.*

The Enlightened Householder

A householder is a person living in the world; working, raising a family, engaging in community. An enlightened householder is one who has come to know the truth and light in their own being, their own GodSelf, so intimately that it infuses their daily life with the presence of the holy. Spirit is imbued in flesh, in word, in deed and this one becomes a Bodhisattva just by living.

Many people live a householder's life which is 'normal' and 'mundane' without any spiritual underpinnings, but they are likely to feel a sense of discontent and dissatisfaction with a life that is *supposed* to feel fulfilling. Life is not really alive if it is not motivated by love and moved by love. When we come to see this by chasing after the peace our heart and soul demands of our life, we are set free from the mundane and live in a state of acute awareness that is effortless and timeless. We are the living incarnation of spirit, conscious of itself as such, but supremely unselfconscious.

The journey from householder to enlightened householder is a journey of returning to the Source, to the soul and essence of our being, and surrendering the reins of life to be led from inner knowing rather than outer thinking. There is nothing wrong with thinking, with the mind or the ego, when they know their right place in the scheme of our being. Our body, mind and ego need to be dethroned and restored to their status as servants of the most high….the most high in us, our soul and the GodSelf which created and animates it.

So, how might one get there? This whole book is a guidemap of sorts, not to enlightenment so much as to the One that enlightens. Turning inward, listening and following, disciplining the senses and the ego-mind to be subservient to the spirit; these are the ways to be restored to inner truth. This path home takes many forms and is the spiritual journey which our souls came to earth to express. We land in the earth, made unconscious by its denseness and unconsciousness, made heavy by the vehicle of flesh that we must come to master. Life teaches us many things and, hopefully, we learn the lessons that awaken us to ourselves as spiritual beings, as did all those saints, sages and mystics before us. Once awakened, we use our vehicle for God's purposes, the purposes of love and consciousness, and become helpers to others who continue to sleepwalk and suffer through the school of earth life.

This is how the enlightened householder helps awaken their brothers and sisters; by embodying truth, light and love and emanating it in daily interactions that are not so much profound as they are subtle and sublime. The receiver of such lessons and blessings may not even fully understand what is taking place; though they may feel that something was odd or unique about the person or the interaction. That there was something deep and meaningful that is juxtaposed to the mundane nature of the exchange.

The enlightened householder becomes as communion for those she serves in this seemingly menial capacity. The exchange transfers love and light and restores life and spirit, even if for a fleeting moment. The sum of these moments act to awaken and enliven the receiver who then turns back toward the Self to seek truth. These informal *teachers* can be found in every walk of life and every community. They seem *wise beyond their years*. They exude quiet confidence and peace. Their calm is contagious and attracting. You may not consciously know why you want to be near this person, this beacon of light, but something in you knows and returns to it for more of the inexplicable presence that soothes you.

Find your practice, find your center, find your peace, soak it in, let it convince you of your divine origin and the source of life which desires to merge with you and flow through you. Do this consistently, thoroughly, until the Knower in you motivates and directs the movement of your spirit, mind, body, actions, words, thoughts....until you become a channel for truth, an enlightened householder who has found their true purpose, whatever form it takes.

When you have eyes to see, you will notice these ones; simple, humble, calm and powerful beings who mirror the truth that resides in you.

What is real?

Cracks in the pavement
and in the sky
As all I once held true
dissolves or smolders
From the periphery
eating its way in toward me
Toward my sense of myself and reality

I try to look away
to no avail
Infiltrating and intruding
the questions arise
Nagging and scratching
at my mind
Demanding consideration and assimilation
What is real?
What is true?
Who are you?
What will you be?
Why are you here?
What will you do?
How do you know….
Once again the footing shakes

no solid ground in sight

Stirrings cause disturbance

peace scatters

Leaving only wonderings

about sanity

Green looking grey today

The destroyer comes to till

the soil beneath

Tearing and crushing clods

that do not serve

Mixing the compost

teeming with worms

To make black gold for the crop

I will forget the questions

I will dig in the dirt

Blacken my nails and hands

Planting the seeds I have

Watching for new shoots

Sprouting from burials deep

Learning the plants as they mature

Simplicity

This Morning

Sun streaming in windows
Peace and contentment in my heart
Freedom of spirit and mind to just be
Icicles dripping effortlessly
Allowing light and warmth to transform them to water
Which will bring us the spring, new life
Glassy, sparkling wonder....purposeless beauty
Dripping, liquid life...quenching thirst, resurrecting verdant landscapes
On the land and in the heart
Blue sky pours color into my eyes and breath into my lungs
Sighing, I am here, I am me, it is enough.

Life is simple, but it is not easy. Not easily understood with the thinking mind, that is. If we were to step back and contemplate the cycles of life, the passing of time, the seasons of nature; if we were to watch closely and show up fully to the magnificence of the physical world, we would see the simple beauty of creation animated by spirit.

Throughout time, humanity has aligned itself with these cycles. In our present time, it seems we are moving toward aligning ourselves with the inter-web of consciousness, the virtual existence that technology has offered us. People have actually spent so much time out of their bodies on the internet that they forget to eat and sustain their physical form in physical ways. Although there is much dysfunction in this phenomenon, it does affirm our ability to have experience without form.

In meditation, we consciously move toward an experience of being without form, without thought, without emotion. As we sink into ourselves, we experience stillness, contentment, and peace which passes understanding when we think of the challenges of our lives and the condition of the world. In this restful place everything becomes simple and clear. The *problems* that weighed down our minds and hearts seem to dissipate as a greater, simpler reality takes over our felt-being. Deep acceptance which blossoms into intimate, exquisite love draws us back into the love relationship between our soul and our Source. We let it. We fall in, thirsty for a drink of these sacred, healing waters; satiated by exposure and absorption.

What matters now? Not time, not work, not problems, not even people. The simple reality of love is a *Oneness* that defies reason. What matters now is love and how we can bring this love experience back to our life in the body; how we can allow the reality of this experience to transform our being, changing our hearts and minds so that true north is directed from inside.

Creating and allowing for simplicity requires that we pare down and let go. If our minds are cluttered, we unclutter them. We use practices like mindfulness, meditation, and concentration, to become masters of the thinking mind; quieting it so we can be. We use practices to calm the emotions which are directed by the thinking mind; reorganizing and reframing our former beliefs to align them with the higher truth of our next experience. We use practices to respect and train the impulses of the body, the temple of our spirit, so that it will be a sound and useful instrument for our journey and the gifts we are meant to bring to the world in our life.

Simplicity is also letting go of matter, detaching from having 'stuff' just for the sake of having it. Our living and working spaces reflect the simplicity or the clutter of our minds and beings. Look around your space. Clean it up and clear it out and then put back only that which nourishes your being, supports your life, and brings you peace. We really need very little but what we do have can support our progress by being beautiful, useful, moderate and comforting. Home is a sanctuary for the spirit, a resting place of nourishment and relaxation. Work is a stage for action and intention; organized, productive, and effective workspace allows us to engage more fully in the tasks at hand, whatever they may be.

We live in a consumerist, capitalist, materialistic culture. It is not easy to unplug and extract ourselves from the myriad options and temptations that present themselves to us daily. It takes some concerted effort to choose, enjoy and love what enhances our lives, and discard, let go of, surrender that which diminishes our lives.

When we have succeeded in simplifying ourselves and our space, we will be able to sink naturally back into the cycles of the seasons, the cycles of life, and enjoy the ebb and flow created for our enjoyment and our education in earth.

Winter Time

The clock is slowing and the light is fading
Time seems to move from liquid to solid as water turns
to ice
Breathing takes up space not noticed before now
and thinking
Sinking into myself as I reflect on the year
Four quick seasons with a breadth of joys
Four tormenting changes as the soul rehabilitates
Settling in now, to my own heartbeat
which I hear without trying
The breath is breathing me as solid melts into solitude
No more good grasp on reality
Ephemeral expansion and dissipation
into simple being
Thank you, winter, for slowing things down
for making it clear that we are not in charge
Thank you time, for your enigmatic flow
that distorts reality so we can see eternity in it.

Sadhana, Sangha, Satsang & Seva

The simple life has a rhythm and a rhyme to it. It is a series of choices, like a good diet, that nourish, enliven and sustain us. Having a *Sadhana* (daily practice), a *Sangha* (spiritual community), and *Satsang* (space/time to contemplate truth) support the simple life. *Seva* is a time of service, of giving of ourselves with no thought of return.

Creating a daily practice is not so difficult. Meditation, prayer, yoga, mindfulness practice, japji/chanting; these can all help us to begin our day centered and re-connected to our innermost truth. It is the attitude in which these practices are performed that makes all the difference. If we make ourselves a list of tasks that *must* be accomplished in order to feel *spiritual* or *successful*, we will be missing the whole point. Sadhana is a daily practice of devotion, using the body, the voice, the heart and the mind to remember and act out the desire of our heart and soul to be connected to God, to ourselves, and to one another.

Finding a community of like-minded people, whether in an ashram, a church, a yoga studio, a book club, 12 Step group, hiking club, is essential to our need for connection, validation and feedback. No man is an island, and no woman. We need one another to support our efforts, mirror the impact we are having on those around us, and walk alongside of us as we make our way into deeper love and greater consciousness. A conscious and connected community that practices and plays together is a life-giving force and a gift from God. Friendships can also act in this way, a Sangha of 2, but an open, accepting and supportive community, Sangha or church will buoy us up for the challenges of the journey and celebrate with us in the successes and joys of life.

Finding a guide or teacher in a book, in the wisdom literature of all traditions, in a human being, a minister, a wise counselor, is a delight for the spirit. Sitting with words and ideas, allowing them to sink into our being, contemplating them and awaiting the deep insights that arise from this practice is like growing a garden of beautiful flowers and watching them go from leafy stalks to glorious blossoms.

Service is the purposeful practice of practical kindness. It expresses the ultimate goal of our soul, having our whole life express itself in service to Love. *Seva* can be accomplished in many ways; giving time, money, attention, kindness, food, shelter, assistance. It is a decision to share, to use our resources in a way that assists others. Whether this is expressed by volunteering, helping your neighbor shovel, buying a meal for a hungry stranger, or offering up your heart in prayer for others; Seva will enrich your life with gratitude and blessings untold as Love begets Love and blessing begets blessing.

Life, Death and Chocolate

What do these three have in common? More than one might imagine.

I am a minister. I work in Hospice. I sit at the line between life and death every day with those who are preparing to cross that line. I am as fully present to this experience as I am to enjoying the very earthly delight of chocolate, one of my guiltless pleasures. The Zen Master, Thich Nhat Hahn says, 'If I do not grow lettuces, I cannot write poetry.' I say, 'If I do not eat chocolate, I cannot help people die.'

Of course, I am using chocolate as a metaphor for the deep enjoyment of the things of life. Nature, beauty, chocolate, good wine, music, sex, art, poetry, people.....all blessings to be engaged fully; mindfully, heartfully, soulfully. Some feel these earthly pleasures are temptations or indulgences, I instead find them to be condolences; the balancing force to carrying the suffering of the world. Deep mindful experience of any lovely or sorrowful thing in life stretches the heart so that it can celebrate joy and alleviate suffering; so it can experience the conditions of life in full remembrance of its harmonious and bittersweet balance. This process matures us, no longer running from pain to seek pleasure, we walk the delicate balance with full acceptance and consciousness of both.

St John of the Cross in 'The Dark Night of the Soul' says that seeking any consolation is not fully giving over to be God's instrument. True as this may be, God gives us consolations freely and readily; friends, books, activities, rest, beauty. Though I am sometimes impatient for the more loving and sweet things of life, God knows exactly which to deliver and when. This perfect and miraculous timing is nothing short of a Lover's kiss, a Lover's voice in my ear whispering, *'Fear not, all is well.'*

Another residual of religious strictures is to deny oneself pleasure. I am not a fan of self-indulgence or over-indulgence, but what God provides me with, I accept gratefully and enjoy fully. *Enjoy* to me means to have joy spring from within you. To me, joy is one of the highest forms of gratitude as it is the heart's spontaneous song of love and thanks, of acknowledgement and praise, of trust and faith, in the God of Goodness and Love.

I have seen people die struggling and afraid, fearful of what comes, holding onto life's regrets and sorrows. I have seen people die at peace, simplified by the process and surrendering to the journey. I have seen people live in both of these ways as well. Dying is the process the body and psyche go through when shutting down to this life. Death is the soul's destination when the earth body has breathed its last. Neither are to be feared, but both are to be prepared for.

The Death Bed

Eyes pierce souls when death is near

Drowning in the reality of mortality

Broken hearts, unfinished dreams, suffering and loss

No more time to pretend

Raw, sharp, deep, real

Honor and blessing to sit in this chair

To dive into these eyes, this life nearly done

Jagged knives rip my heart in the presence of this pain

Soothing peace rolls over the gushing wounds as love is born

In this moment of truth, in this communion

In which one is seen and one is seer

His words find my ears, 'Comfort the sick and dying.'

I serve my master and my neighbor at once

Suffering and gratitude mix in the salty, watery tears that arise

Your will, not mine.

We have been given many instruction books on living and dying. It would be wise to take them into account and practice these parts of life that our pain-shy culture avoids at all cost. Whatever one's belief system, there is plenty of historical, anecdotal evidence for the existence of an afterlife of one form or another. I am not a fan of the 'heaven or hell' dichotomy, nor have I seen a self-professed nihilist die peacefully. Our psyche does not take well to the possibility of uselessness and extinction, especially as death draws near. Terror replaces the idea that we are done when life is done, that life itself has no meaning. Science has us continue as energy which cannot be created or destroyed; religion has us continue as soul, stepping into an afterlife whose purpose and experience differs depending on the belief system.

People say that *no one can know what happens after death*. I find this a bold statement as many have experienced medical death and return to tell of it. And many, like myself, have had many experiences straddling the great divide between living and dying; acting as midwives for souls as they vacate their dying bodies, and redirecting those who have already lost theirs. When I speak of death, dying and spirits, I speak from years of experience which I did not ask for but have acclimated to. Here is one example...

*~**Aunt Ethel** spent the last years of her life lying in a hospital bed in her kitchen. Her kitchen was iconic in our family with the old silver handled fridge with bulbous rounded corners, coal black wood cook stove, aluminum sided kitchen table with lime green patterned*

top, cast iron heat grate on the floor in the parlor, feather mattresses, storage rooms piled high with treasures.

The day came when the whole, wide family came to Ethel's house for her passing; some 40 of us as she was one of six siblings and I one of over 20 grandchildren. She was what I would later learn is called 'minimally responsive'. She breathed a shallow and almost silent breath while family arrived with food, children, noise...gathering in her parlor and living room. I was about 25 and somewhat stunned at what was happening. Once again, hordes of people but little connection. I saw fear in the eyes of her children and sorrow in the eyes of her mother and then I saw busyness....eating, talking, laughing. No hushed tones or respect for the dying. I moved toward the kitchen and stood at the end of her bed. Two of my aunts were the only others in the room with me as she took her last breath, my first experience of the death rattle. I felt panic for a single sharp moment....and then I saw and felt her spirit leave her body with her breath and blast out into the room in every direction, and right through my being. It was the unmistakable presence of Aunt Ethel whom I loved...but now she was free, joyful and light. Now she was part of me as she deposited this last ethereal hug on my soul before moving on to the great beyond. I could not cry for her or for myself. I felt strangely alienated from my family and strangely bonded to my aunts, Charlotte and Miny, who were in the kitchen with me at that moment. I didn't ask them if they felt it too. Aunt Miny said I should go get Ethel's kids and husband so I did....in a daze of awesome wonder and sweetness I delivered the news that she was dead. What a strange mixture of feelings to share a single moment in time. I saw Ethel again at the funeral, and Harold at his funeral, and Jim and Joel and many, many other spirits as I went on to be a Priest, Hospice Chaplain and bereavement counselor years later. I believe that Ethel's gift drew me back toward God, toward life beyond the worldly way of living, to a mission of guiding souls toward the great truth that the soul outlives the flesh and that there is freedom in it....that there is a home for it beyond earthlife. Dead people seem to find me now....and when they do, I direct them into the Light of God and they are enveloped in it. I am a simple crossing-guard for their spirit, but they often return with tales of the sweet life and messages for those left behind. ~

Though not everyone has these kinds of experiences, that any of us do is a wonder and a grace. When we share our experiences, we bring strength and hope to those who are in fear and doubt. Every person has a gift to share; story, music, art, song, humor, poetry, tenderness, experience. Our gifts connect us on the level of the heart to those in a body and to those who have left the body behind for a time. There need not be fear or mystery in that.

Dead folks

Coming to be seen, to be directed
Spirits lost in the ethers
Afraid, angry, sad, they await me
Appearing when they like, or when I call to them
The slightest thought evokes their presence
No time and space to travel, mind is the beacon
Heart the messenger, calling them to me
Did they never hear, 'Go to the light'
Were they never told, 'It's ok to go'
Do they not know the name of God, in any form
They come to me, like moths to flame
I feel them, hear them, see them
In their watery, silvery form
That causes shivers and standing hair
And open heart that desires their peace
I send them home to the great beyond
Mysterious to some, but known and knowable
With the confidence of experience I point the way
And call the escort who seems my muse
So quickly He responds to this poor and mighty soul
Commanding the heavens with compassion
I do not ask, 'Why me?' I see, I serve, I move along
Muse for the heavens in return

Knowing grace will provide and protect

Knowing the mightier force from which I sprang

Knowing peace when the day is done and the spirits rest

Reabsorbed by the light and the love that lovers seek

And I remain, in this rough world, stranded

In sight of the other but not in reach of it

Dutifully awaiting my time of reunion

With impatience and impudence

God smiles at me, and I smile back

My epitaph will read 'Crossing guard.'

Victory over death, my reward.

Transformation

'If you use your mind to try to and understand reality,
you will understand neither your mind nor reality. If
you try and understand reality without using your mind,
you will understand both your mind and reality.'

~*Bodhidharma*

How do we wake up to spirit and stay awake? Religion, spirituality, philosophy, belief, science ....they have all assisted us in opening and raising our consciousness; evolving the consciousness of the planet in this most auspicious age in which we live. The turn of the century, the new millennium, the Age of Acquarius, technology, quantum physics, string theory; these have brought us closer to deciphering and describing a *theory of everything.* I see this as humans beginning to catch up with the interconnected, interbeing of God. Wisdom literature like the Bible describes it as, '*In God, we live and move and have our being.'* The transformation takes place not in growing into this reality, but in becoming consciously aware of it.

Our human thinking minds are as closed circuits, gated gardens, enclosed by us to separate, own and defend our sense of self. When we open the circuit and the gate, we see that our small being which we considered a free-standing cell, is, in fact, connected to all that is; one point of consciousness in the interplay of interbeing. When we allow this idea to become a reality through an experience of ourselves beyond mind, we begin to transform, to *'make a thorough and dynamic change in form, appearance or character'* in the way we experience ourselves and life.

The visionary artist, Alex Gray, created a series of life-size paintings called 'Sacred Mirrors'. I like to use his images to bring this point home. He paints human subjects from the outside in; from skin, to muscles, to organs, circulatory system, and then to more and more subtle aspects of our existence. Once the physical layers are peeled away, he goes on to paint our psychic/energetic/chakra system, our spiritual/etheric/ soul energy, and finally the union of the one to the infinite *Universal Mind Lattice*.

**Please find the artwork of Alex Grey at
http://alexgrey.com/art/paintings/sacred-mirrors/
Psychic Energy System
Spiritual Energy System
Universal Mind Lattice**

http://alexgrey.com/art/paintings/sacred-mirrors/

The transformation comes in experiencing ourselves in the full spectrum of consciousness and energy that we are, and gaining in facility with moving across this continuum as needed in our earthly experience. The spirit informs and guides the flesh; the flesh perceives and experiences the earthly life. The splendor of the feedback loop of divine/human/divine understanding and experience is the journey from the mundane to the sublime. We are here in physical form to express spirit as truly and consistently as possible. When we are deposited into the flesh, there is a veil of forgetting while we acclimate to the conditions of this planet and then reawaken to the awesome knowledge and truth that we are spiritual beings having a human experience, aware of both and inextricable from the source of life; inextricable from connection to and communion with God and all other parts of creation.

The transformation, the thorough change in character, happens when we allow ourselves to have experience beyond thought. The thinking mind is a limited tool. Even our language does not adequately describe the experiences of the spirit. When we read the mystic writings and poetry of Rumi, St Francis, Hafiz, Basho, we catch a glimpse of this reality which may ignite the spark of remembrance in our spirit and urge us toward the full consciousness of this reality.

Philosophy

The love of wisdom
The study of meaning
Who knows or cares
Mind out of time or time out of mind
Which is living?

Mind steals away hours and days
Bereft of satisfaction, of contentment
Mental masturbation pleasures itself
While moments slip away
Never to be seen again

Time, a sequence of moments
Exquisitely felt joy or suffering
Exquisitely experienced beauty or horror
Sharp, deep, visceral, sweet
Being, lacking meaning but not wisdom

And so we dance the dance of fools
Lost in now or then
Contradiction or complement
Paradox or chaos
Fate or destiny
Truth or illusion

Transition

Change, oh tumultuous friend
That wreaks havoc for who knows what sake
Our Lord moves heaven and earth
While we try to steer clear of danger
Forgetting that all that arises is love
Of one form or another, patient and pure
Guiding our souls deeper into wisdom
As life teaches us all that is true

This dance does not belong to us
Though will and might can bend and slow
The progress that we could have made
Had we surrendered to its flow
We must concede to the Almighty
Whose strength will not be marred by man
And though we fancy ourselves so bright
We are but shadows cast by light

Until the day we are restored
To that true Source which is our home
The nature of this life in us
Comes forth with a force that is its own
Its course is set if we but yield
Allowing the graceful movement its way

Behold the jewel of Jesus' crown
Chiseled by days and tears and love

Peace at last, and quiet pain
Suffered for those who stray so far
Intent on gathering souls of men
To be restored to the northern star
Shaded eyes and muffled ears
Keep the truth from shining in
From welling up from depths unknown
To mortal men whose eyes are closed

When, my Lords, will Light shine forth
In fullness and intensity
When will hearts break hardness down
Melting into this joyful stream
Where love alone guides everything

SECTION III:

<u>PEACE</u>

Let it be.

This Morning

Sun streaming in windows

Peace and contentment in my heart

Freedom of spirit and mind to just be

Icicles dripping effortlessly

Allowing light and warmth to transform them to water

Which will bring us the spring, new life

Glassy, sparkling wonder....purposeless beauty

Droplets, liquid life...quenching thirst, resurrecting verdant landscapes

On the land and in the heart

Blue sky pours color into my eyes and breath into my lungs

Sighing, I am here, I am me, it is enough.

How to be. How to be enough. Being and becoming in tandem as we love, accept, stretch, grow; being again something greater yet simpler. This is the evolutionary pattern of life. We, as created beings, are held in the graceful stream of love; now tossed, now turned, floating on the surface or pulled to the depths by a force we cannot see or anticipate. All of it is useful to Love. All of it has obvious or unseen purpose. That old cliché, *'Everything happens for a reason.'* is true….that's why it has lasted so long. Do we have the patience and faith in Life to await the understanding that arises after the experience?

As any human, I sometime rebel and rail against how God chooses to teach us, to stretch us. I see the felt pain and suffering of human kind in illness, death, loss and grief. I see humans being humbled by hardships and traumatized by the hell that is war, in its many forms. My heart aches and breaks for their suffering; for theirs, for yours, for my own. I let it break, though I am not always graceful about it.

When I have dying patients who express grace and acceptance in the process of dying; in the pain, the loss, the discomfort, I pray to take on some of that simple, trusting beauty by the time my time comes. My inner reaction to witnessing pain can be juvenile or adolescent at best, as I feel deeply the pain of others but move toward frustration, anger or despair for not being able to alleviate it, stop it. And so surrender and acceptance are my lesson, our lesson.

Of course, if one is *fighting* an illness, then fight with all your might. But when the time comes that fighting is futile, when there is no longer the desire nor the energy with which to continue, the great surrender is all that is left.

In living as in dying, there are points at which we must come to just let be what is. Times to watch for God's will and flow along with it to the destination that cannot be seen round the bend of the stream. My good friend, Lou, says, *'It is what it is.'* This, his philosophy for getting through life and continuing to love in the face of illness, surgery, cancer treatment, family dynamics. He sits at the bedside of dying patients and strums his mountain dulcimer to offer his talent and his heart for those who are closer to life's end than himself. He loves the innocent genuineness of the side of the deathbed as I do. This common denominator, this ever present reminder of our own mortality. None of us get out of this place alive. That is what is true. It is what it is. How about we do this together?

Let it Be

When I find myself in times of trouble,
Mother Mary come to me
Speaking words of wisdom, let it be
And in my hour of darkness,
She is standing right in front of me
Speaking words of wisdom, let it be

Let it be, let it be
Let it be, let it be
Whisper words of wisdom, let it be

And when the broken hearted people
Living in the world agree
There will be answer, let it be
For though they may be parted
There is still a chance that they will see
There will be answer let it be

Let it be, let it be
Let it be, let it be
There will be an answer, let it be

And when the night is cloudy
There is still a light that shines on me
Shine on 'til tomorrow, let it be
I wake up to the sound of music,
Mother Mary comes to me
Speaking words of wisdom, let it be
Let it be, let it be
Let it be, yeah, let it be
Whisper words of wisdom, let it be

~The Beatles

Constant Craving

Dead to this world

I am as dead to this world

The mind and musings of humankind bore and pain me

Driven to distraction from the one voice that matters

The soul seeks silence and beauty, touch and love

Authenticity is essential for beingness

I sit in the woods and write

I can breathe here….my soul is resuscitated

'Look, eat, rest.' it whispers to my strained, trained mind

'Stop, breathe, be.'

The wind sings to me, the sun kisses me,

A surge of love inflames my heart

God takes me from the world of sorrows into His breast

Into the beating heart that speaks only love, and peace, and goodness

I am made from this

Restored to myself by His call to the peaceful woods

As the soul before me who fled to Walden

To remember and to be

The yearning of the heart; the empty, hollow space that draws us like a magnet, is not our own longing alone. Life is calling to itself. God is calling to itself; nagging and cajoling us to return to what's most true and most real. This constant craving feels as much a curse as a blessing as it will not allow us to rest on our laurels in a semi-wakeful state. It is sent to disturb; to *'interfere with the normal arrangement or functioning.'*

Normal' is such an overrated and overly sought after existence. In mathematics, it is simply the space where the most number of people land on any particular characteristic. The herd mentality, following like lemmings, trying to *'belong'* to some small thing that makes the ego feel safe and secure. Peer pressure, tradition pressure, culture pressure, gender pressure, fashion, fads, comparing. Humans spend so much time and effort trying to *fit in* that they lose track of the unique and wondrous creation that they are, that we are, that you are.

When we step out of this rat race, we feel bereft of community and compadres for a time, but we also have some freedom to re-acclimate to our own sense of self and heart. In our hearts, beyond all cravings for belonging, is the great desire to know ourselves and express our potential to the highest degree possible while living in the earth in this time in this body. This is the *life purpose* that so many seek, but it cannot be found among the throngs of autonomatons. We must take a season away for reflection and recomposition. We must turn inward to the constant craving that will not give us rest until it is addressed thoroughly and completely, until it is the altruistic and all-knowing *boss of us*, by our request and our permission.

Then begins the lifelong conversation with Soul, with Self, with God….who am I? …..what am I here for? ……what shall I do today to express the beingness that I am? Now the dance begins between the inner divine and the outer mundane. A dance that is sweet and joyful, surprising and delightful, strenuous and simple. Staying in the conversation is the practice, the commitment; following the inner guidance and direction is the vow.

And what of me?

What will you ask of me, dear Lord
Which form shall I take to glorify your name?
Mother, sister, chaplain, friend, teacher, preacher
Why the intrigue? My spirit thirsts for your word
Tell me straight and strong, I pray
Loud and clear that I may not stray
From your dictum, your desire,
As my petty life would do
Slipping and sleeping when your flock needs tending
Distracted by fool's gold
Clarify my sight, make it a holy one
Keep me close, my Christ, that I might serve you well
In all good and holy things
Simple and innocent in your sight
And useful to your cause

~I took a walk in the woods with God this morning. My angsty, rebellious personality not happy, but compelled. Thinking I should sit in meditation, thinking I should pray and offer up the Eucharist for the sake of the world. I set out alone on the dirt road that leads to more and more rustic paths into deeper and darker woods. I pray the Chaplet of Divine Mercy on my prayer beads until God tells me to stop. 'Can't we just have a talk?' is the question that arises from the still well inside, surfacing like an air bubble into my mind in words as clear as bells. I smile to myself and surrender again to the perfection of Self, of God in me, who knows me and puts up with my strange, impatient humanity.

God shows me the beauty of the path, revealing all the sweet things that make this heart sing....moss and ferns, babbling brook, dappled sunlight, dew on leaves, sweetly singing breeze.

My mind is hushed and my spirit restored in this beauty, at once delicate and harsh as lichen devour a fallen log, as branches pruned by wind clutter the way. I step over them deftly and without fear, maneuvering around puddles and mud, taking care over slippery rocks, ever following the path uphill and down, in and out of sunbeams that warm me to the core. God speaks to me with every step, assuring me of the rightness of this path for me, reminding me of what I have learned about wise maneuvering and steady walking; about the safety of the path and the darkness in the woods beyond, where I hear a tree fall and look to see it has been pushed over by a bear. I am turned back by fear; adrenaline rushing into my body, mind scrambling to make sense....repeating the riddle, 'If a tree falls in the woods when no one is listening, does it make any sound?'

Smiling through the chemical survival instinct dumped into my bloodstream, I smile again to myself and let God pull me from the deep woods back to the sweetly wooded, dappled path; back to the sweet conversation reassuring me that this is where I belong, walking along with those God sends me, pointing out the dapples of light on the way to bring hope, pointing out the puddles and mud and slippery stones to avoid pitfalls, stopping in the rays of sun that nourish and convalesce.

God tells me I am a shepherd, an innocent who knows the path and can guide others upon it. I am not the one called to blaze trails in the dark woods, I am not the one to wrestle bears and demons. I as a shepherd, one of many, who guides gently, providing solace and milk and honey for the lambs of God. I see that stained glass window again, the one from the church I grew up in, the one that convinced me that I am as a lamb held in the arms of Christ, beloved and protected.

I continue my walk, asking God if I have failed Love; if I was meant to be a deep woods, demon-wrestler; if this woodland path is somehow a demotion from my former path. God assures me that I have been transferred but not demoted, that Love needs me here; that the innocent heart in me is just the right medicine for those suffering souls who seek comfort and hope. God's smile warms me from the depths of my being as I see myself as God sees me; as I accept what He says, what She requests of me. I am not obliged or commanded, but thoroughly convinced; content in the knowing that my crooked path has been and will continue to be useful to God and to the souls I serve on God's behalf, in the name of Love. ~

Each of us have a path to walk. Each of us will have others set before us to guide, and we will be guided by God, nourished by God, loved by God, for our willingness to serve. Each of us will have a constant craving to do the will of the Love that springs forth from our being. That craving is satiated by acceptance of the mission, presence to the task, and surrender to the flow of life and love. We do not always get to see the fruits of our labors, but our good and trusting hearts receive more than enough feedback, blessing and reward to continue on our way without having to know all or see all. Life unfolds in every direction at once depending on the will of God and the cooperation of humankind and nature. We will not see the whole of the path stretching out before us, but neither will we be bereft of preparation and companionship as we walk along. The constant craving for union with this Companion, for surrender to it and consumption by it, keeps us moving along until the appointed time when we leave this world behind and return to our Source for that Ultimate Reunion.

Divine Romance

Divine Romance

The sweet love of Christ pours into my heart again
Overwhelming thought, reason, worry
Liquid gold, honey and light swallow me whole
Heart and mind burst open in simple, profound love
What more is there? What more do I need?
Nothing. No books, no knowledge, no opinions, no questions
Fully satiated by the Presence and the Truth
I care not what the world imagines of this holy madness
The sweet embrace of Christ's heart into which I melt, merge, disappear
It is all I can see, all I care about. I am consumed;
I am extinguished and set afire in the same instant
Made one with the lover of my soul, communion in essence
Who will believe such grace has descended upon me, a poor sinner? Who will be convinced by my reverie?
I care not, Jesus is in me and I in Him
A smile appears on my face, erupting from a heart burst open in love
Exquisite, ecstatic love....it's all I see
What comes of it is Christ's concern
I let myself be lost in this divine romance.
I let myself be.

The Kiss of the Lord

The kiss of the Lord leaves all human cares satisfied
One cannot remember the day there was want
The sweetness and light arouse sublime splendor
That ripples through matter, making it dissolve

No longer flesh and bone, but electric fire and light
Vibration so intense yet subtle
How does man describe ecstacy?

Words do not do justice to this ultimate romance
Where love meets soul with no separation
Fleshly pleasures wane
The heart expands to fill the universe in exquisite,
intimate union.

He Has Me

That Voice called to my soul and would not halt its calling

That flame draws the moth to itself, ignoring all former ties

The One Tie, the one, inseparable connection placed before spirit took on form

The primary union forgotten but not gone

His Voice awakens a remembrance beyond reason. I fly toward it.

Things, people, fall away as the tractor beam of Truth pulls me to Itself

It is beyond will, beyond desire, this annihilating force,

Which strips me of all life, all breath, save His own which sustains me

My senses have the taste for Him alone, all other pleasures lose their savor

This urgent passion draws me deeper, bereft of a resting place save His Heart.

He is a jealous lover. He would have me completely.

Quiet hours

In quiet hours
I remember you to my Lord
You who suffer and are sorrowful
You who are sick and dying
You who grieve
In quiet hours
I pour out my heart
To my sweet, benevolent Christ
To comfort and strengthen and spare you
To lift you up and hold you
In tender arms
And moreso still for those who seem complete
Whose lives look good, but whose hearts weep
The silent tears of loneliness
Of prideful hearts too hard to break
For fear of crumbling into dust
Erased by wind

And so these quiet hours go
Conversing with my God who knows
The deep desire of my heart
For all to know what He doth brought
The solace of the wretched
Salvation's peace

SECTION IV:

<u>MYSTICAL POETRY</u>

in order of appearance

What to say

My heart yearns to share truth, to awaken hearts

What to say

Words like rivers flow from the minds and pens of the ages

What more to say

Sounding the call of the spirit again in this age, through this mind, with this pen

What left to say

Drunk on the sweetness of being

Love, clear and present

Breath, soft and rhythmic

Skin, alive and perceptive

What is that other we call life

That race, that mask, that noise

Deep silence drowns it out

Leaving depth without sound

Feeling without pretense

Heart without guards, without guile

Sweet tears of relief and joy

Simpleton at peace

Say that.

Knowing

Some truths are deeply seated and unalterable

Standing the test of time, fate and the movement of the stars

Under all that seems real but is illusion

This solid force remains unchanged

We lose ourselves to it taking on flesh

And are rstored to it in awakening to life

Wisdom informing this body/mind

At once mundane and sublime

Natural reminders surround us, poking at our drowsy spirits

Sights and smells and feelings and touch

Deepened to ecstacy when seen from eternity

This world is a stage

Some sleepwalk, some awaken to play their part

In love and amusement, allowing the play to unfold

Merrily, merrily and with open heart

Taking in the joy with the sorrow, the ebb with the flow

The waxing with the waning, the union with the waiting

Urgency dissolves in presence

Peace pervades the parade

Simplicity allows for free flowing movement

Sweetness drips from the I

Sweetness and light

hard heart

the pains our hearts endure
with battle scars twisting scar tissue
until no love can enter in
minute spaces imprisoned in iron shackles
of fear and loneliness

how shall we pry open this hard heart
resuscitate it and peel away the thick, leather straps
that block the natural and dynamic flow
barbed and spitting warnings to steer clear
angsty, impotent, indiscriminate jabs

all guards are up, shields raised
as if love were a threat to health, to peace
when lack of love is a living hell disguised as calm
set one spark near that dry tinder
and the flames of Hades spring forth

self-preservation is a farse
one cannot be preserved from life
it moves of its own accord and has its way
no matter our rebellion or seeming protection
surrender is the only choice

control is futile and bogus

and oh when gloves are off and guard is down
the sweet torment of love takes hold
a torrent of movement and grace
unmasking all parts, returned to nakedness
vulnerable, tender, afraid are we....of what
of being who we were meant to be

oh sore, soft heart that chooses life
stay open and take the jabs of the fearful
only love prevails in the end
after all the tears and heartache subside
peace, hope, joy remain to encourage and revive

I Am That

I Am That, the sweet, good wave of love and life
I Am That, the depth that has no end and no beginning
Not separate from life, from movement, from illusion
But maker of the dream in mind which tangles and
hides
Come out, wherever you are,
Come out and in, into the deep place where peace lives
Where you dwell, and where you sprang from
You are returning without leaving
Reuniting without dividing, without separating
How strange and true this trick of Self
Awakening to the game as the Game Master
How subtle the view from here, filmy shadows
No weight or sound, phantasms that convince, delude
Search no more, you are That too
Victory over the world, over time
Eternity is here
Praise be to Christ, the great I AM.

The Eucharist

Holy Sacrament that restores me to Life
Daily bread infused with Grace
I call upon my Lord to move heaven and earth
To make the elixir that erases sin

He moves and makes His Presence known
A bolt of Love, a breeze of peace
The air rarified as I intone
The command that brings His blessed hand

Like lightening to a lightening rod
The force of will and devotion
Draws down His precious gift
Given to me, and through me, to them

Whoever wants His grace receives
Through hands and feet made right by Him
The blessed feast which knows no end
Blood and body in this servant's hands.

And oh, what crazy joy to serve
The feast of feasts that rescues souls
From darkness' clutch and Satan's bands
That tie the soul to sin and dust

Oh, make us new, my Holy Prince,
Make us ever more like you
Transfixed by Love and saved by Grace
We walk the earth to do your will.

Light unceasing and increasing
Ecstatic union with the Most High
Flesh made new and heart made pure
The Sacred Mystery shines from our eyes.

Whose house is this?

This is my house
I will choose the furniture and curtains
I will paint the walls as I choose
I will leave it clean or messy

I am not in need of guidance
My choices teach me all I need to know
What brings peace, I will repeat
What brings turmoil, I will reject

I am the master of this house
It does not need a manager or doctor
It needs my attentive care and love
To choose what suits me truly

Is there another who can answer
What is the best choice for me
For the house in which I live and rest
The sanctuary of my heart and soul

No…..it is I alone who choose
I alone who decide such things
Guided by history and honest friends
Spurred on by hope and a desire to grow

My capacious heart will be my guide
I will protect its right to choose
I will keep it open in spite of dangers
I will fill my house with song

And those who hear my music will dance along
In my house….the one I build….the one I love
And there will be rejoicing and praise
For all that is good within and without

And peace will reign there
Peace and joy and gratitude
In this house of mine
In this heart of mine

My brother's keeper

How do you entrust my brother to me? my sister?
You have seen my imperfections and trials
You know my hard-hearted and hard-headed ways
And yet you place before me one more wounded than I
More broken and destitute
And you ask my assistance

Counting my blessings and pulling on bootstraps
I turn with compassionate heart
To ease the suffering I see
Though I know not how its done
A simple desire, a simple presence, a simple prayer
I offer myself as an instrument of whatever grace may
flow through me
Not by my merit but by your mercy
And I am in awe, in wonder of the wonders that occur
As one heart feels seen and received by another
As one soul's thirst is quenched by love
I offer my heart for such purposes
Though I know not where the strength will come from
Where the words will come from
I offer myself, blind and dumb, weak and weary
To be a water-bearer for the parched souls of the dying,
the lonely, the desparate

I offer my unworthy heart, my selfish heart

That your blessing might bless me as it passes to my brother

That I also might be healed and made whole in your sight, by your sight

And some miracle of relief occurs, though no circumstance has changed

Love has been communicated, received and returned

Both restored by its eternal truth

If They Only Knew

Shall I reply in outward form when blind ones cannot see past the dark attire which absorbs the sins and sorrows of man?

Shall I shed Light once again by tearing open my chest to bear the joyful treasure that God has placed therein?

Shall I testify to the ecstasy which is God in my flesh?

What gems and treasures must I bear, that God's sweet love has given me?

Intimate gifts, sublime and pure.

What words have I this mortal mouth, this stifling mind, to spread the wings of heaven's song for those to hear who cannot hear?

My flesh afire with holy love; my heart enlarged and burning.

God's mind in every cell of my being; alive, vibrant and tantalizing me to lose myself inside the great sea of sweetness and light that sits just behind my eyes and under my skin.

If not for the sweet call of my Lord to love the people as I am loved, I would surrender to the union which nullifies me and glorifies Thee.

Do they know, can they know, will they know the supernatural beauty and bliss that I am?

I know not how my flesh retains form.

I know not how my flesh continues to obey the laws of earth.

Only by God's grace and command do I remain here.

Angels holding me fast so I do not fly away home as yet.

innocence

the simple sweetness of the heart
no complications or ruminations
that formless space that knows truth
without tethers to the world

what now, rest and love and joy
as time passes and I stand still
open to the freshness of each moment
as God delivers life to me and me to life

returning now and again and now
when forgetting clouds my sight
to the Self that is wide open
simple, discerning, wise

and what joy to share God in me
present in each moment to what arises
heat and light and cool soft breeze
passing over the full emptiness of my being

show only that and all are blessed
by that simple truth that gives us rest
in the spirit of God, of life and love
we remain as one

The Offering

Whatever your heart needs to say to your God, say it
With few words or many, with form or not
God reads between lines and letters and in the silence
The deep desire of your heart to join with Love
Fear not that you do not know the way
God has never left you

Offer your heart and know it is heard, seen, known
Let fly the deep truths and sorrows that you hold
Let love be restored in your soul that you might walk
more lightly
Filled with the peace of Love's presence in you
Now you have been set free of fear
Restored to innocence and wonder

Open Heart

Remain open, heart of mine, regardless of the weather
outside or inside. Remain soft and malleable to love, no
tethers holding one fast, no anchors slowing the flow.
Remember, oh heart, the hardened days, when nothing
moved beyond the gate that held us fast. Remember
and stay open to the simple beauty of love and life
moving through and having its way. Sometimes gentle
other times thrashing, life's movement and seasons
continue. Where will we go from here, no way of
knowing....only trusting in love's goodness. Stay open,
heart of mine, for the joys and sorrows that lie ahead.
Stay open and let it have its way with you, the threshing
floor that hulls the stalk, revealing life-giving grain,
ground to nourish more hearts. Tears and blood, heat
and light pour in to make the holy bread that saves.
Make it in me, oh heart of gold, that human kind may
find its rest and take in love. Oh then the sweetness will
arise, in joy and light as new life enters, restored to that
inner celestial home with rejoicing and peace.

What is real?

Cracks in the pavement
and in the sky
As all I once held true
dissolves or smolders
From the periphery
eating its way in toward me
Toward my sense of myself and reality
I try to look away
to no avail
Infiltrating and intruding
the questions arise
Nagging and scratching
at my mind
Demanding consideration and assimilation
What is real?
What is true?
Who are you?
What will you be?
Why are you here?
What will you do?
How do you know....
Once again the footing shakes
no solid ground in sight

Stirrings cause disturbance
peace scatters
Leaving only wonderings
about sanity
Green looking grey today

The destroyer comes to till
the soil beneath
Tearing and crushing clods
that do not serve
Mixing the compost
teeming with worms
To make black gold for the crop

I will forget the questions
I will dig in the dirt
Blacken my nails and hands
Planting the seeds I have
Watching for new shoots
Sprouting from burials deep
Learning the plants as they mature

This Morning

Sun streaming in windows

Peace and contentment in my heart

Freedom of spirit and mind to just be

Icicles dripping effortlessly

Allowing light and warmth to transform them to water

Which will bring us the spring, new life

Glassy, sparkling wonder….purposeless beauty

Dripping, liquid life…quenching thirst, resurrecting verdant landscapes

On the land and in the heart

Blue sky pours color into my eyes and breath into my lungs

Sighing, I am here, I am me, it is enough.

Winter Time

The clock is slowing and the light is fading
Time seems to move from liquid to solid as water turns
to ice
Breathing takes up space not noticed before now
and thinking
Sinking into myself as I reflect on the year
Four quick seasons with a breadth of joys
Four tormenting changes as the soul rehabilitates
Settling in now, to my own heartbeat
which I hear without trying
The breath is breathing me as solid melts into solitude
No more good grasp on reality
Ephemeral expansion and dissipation
into simple being
Thank you, winter, for slowing things down
for making it clear that we are not in charge
Thank you time, for your enigmatic flow
that distorts reality so we can see eternity in it.

The Death Bed

Eyes pierce souls when death is near

Drowning in the reality of mortality

Broken hearts, unfinished dreams, suffering and loss

No more time to pretend

Raw, sharp, deep, real

Honor and blessing to sit in this chair

To dive into these eyes, this life nearly done

Jagged tears rip my heart in the presence of this pain

Soothing peace rolls over the gushing wounds as love is
born

In this moment of truth, in this communion

In which one is seen and one is seer

His words find my ears, 'Comfort the sick and dying.'

I serve my master and my neighbor at once

Suffering and gratitude mix in the salty, watery tears
that arise

Your will, not mine.

Dead folks

Coming to be seen, to be directed
Spirits lost in the ethers
Afraid, angry, sad, they await me
Appearing when they like, or when I call to them
The slightest thought evokes their presence
No time and space to travel, mind is the beacon
Heart the messenger, calling them to me
Did they never hear, 'Go to the light'
Were they never told, 'It's ok to go'
Do they not know the name of God, in any form
They come to me, like moths to flame
I feel them, hear them, see them
In their watery, silvery form
That causes shivers and standing hair
And open heart that desires their peace
I send them home to the great beyond
Mysterious to some, but known and knowable
With the confidence of experience I point the way
And call the escort who seems my muse
So quickly He responds to this poor and mighty soul
Commanding the heavens with compassion
I do not ask, 'Why me?' I see, I serve, I move along
Muse for the heavens in return

Knowing grace will provide and protect
Knowing the mightier force from which I sprang
Knowing peace when the day is done and the spirits rest
Reabsorbed by the light and the love that lovers seek
And I remain, in this rough world, stranded
In sight of the other but not in reach of it
Dutifully awaiting my time of reunion
With impatience and impudence
God smiles at me, and I smile back
My epitath will read 'Crossing guard.'
Victory over death, my reward.

Philosophy

The love of wisdom
The study of meaning
Who knows or cares
Mind out of time or time out of mind
Which is living?

Mind steals away hours and days
Bereft of satisfaction, of contentment
Mental masturbation pleasures itself
While moments slip away
Never to be seen again

Time, a sequence of moments
Exquisitely felt joy or suffering
Exquisitely experienced beauty or horror
Sharp, deep, visceral, sweet
Being, lacking meaning but not wisdom

And so we dance the dance of fools
Lost in now or then
Contradiction or complement
Paradox or chaos
Fate or destiny
Truth or illusion

Transition

Change, oh tumultuous friend
That wreaks havoc for who knows what sake
Our Lord moves heaven and earth
While we try to steer clear of danger
Forgetting that all that arises is love
Of one form or another, patient and pure
Guiding our souls deeper into wisdom
As life teaches us all that is true

This dance does not belong to us
Though will and might can bend and slow
The progress that we could have made
Had we surrendered to its flow
We must concede to the Almighty
Whose strength will not be marred by man
And though we fancy ourselves so bright
We are but shadows cast by light

Until the day we are restored
To that true Source which is our home
The nature of this life in us
Comes forth with a force that is its own
Its course is set if we but yield

Allowing the graceful movement its way
Behold the jewel of Jesus' crown
Chiseled by days and tears and love

Peace at last, and quiet pain
Suffered for those who stray so far
Intent on gathering souls of men
To be restored to the northern star
Shaded eyes and muffled ears
Keep the truth from shining in
From welling up from depths unknown
To mortal men whose eyes are closed

When, my Lords, will Light shine forth
In fullness and intensity
When will hearts break hardness down
Melting into this joyful stream
Where love alone guides everything

Dead to this world

I am as dead to this world

The mind and musings of humankind bore and pain me

Driven to distraction from the one voice that matters

The soul seeks silence and beauty, touch and love

Authenticity is essential for beingness

I sit in the woods and write

I can breathe here….my soul is resuscitated

'Look, eat, rest.' it whispers to my strained, trained mind

'Stop, breathe, be.'

The wind sings to me, the sun kisses me,

A surge of love inflames my heart

God takes me from the world of sorrows into His breast

Into the beating heart that speaks only love, and peace, and goodness

I am made from this

Restored to myself by His call to the peaceful woods

As the soul before me who fled to Walden

To remember and to be

And what of me?

What will you ask of me, dear Lord
Which form shall I take to glorify your name?
Mother, sister, chaplain, friend
Why the intrigue? My spirit thirsts for your word
Tell me straight and strong, I pray
Loud and clear that I may not stray
From your dictum, your desire,
As my petty life would do
Slipping and sleeping when your flock needs tending
Distracted by fool's gold
Clarify my sight, make it a holy one
Keep me close, my Christ, that I might serve you well
In all good and holy things
Simple and innocent in Your sight
And useful to Your cause

Divine Romance

The sweet love of Christ pours into my heart again
Overwhelming thought, reason, worry
Liquid gold, honey and light swallow me whole
Heart and mind burst open in simple, profound love
What more is there? What more do I need?
Nothing. No books, no knowledge, no opinions, no questions
Fully satiated by the Presence and the Truth
I care not what the world imagines of this holy madness
The sweet embrace of Christ's heart into which I melt, merge, disappear
It is all I can see, all I care about. I am consumed;
I am extinguished and set afire in the same instant
Made one with the lover of my soul, communion in essence
Who will believe such grace has descended upon me, a poor sinner?
Who will be convinced by my reverie?
I care not, Jesus is in me and I in Him
A smile appears on my face, erupting from a heart burst open in love
Exquisite, ecstatic love....it's all I see
What comes of it is Christ's concern
I let myself be lost in this divine romance.
I let myself be.

The Kiss of the Lord

The kiss of the Lord leaves all human cares satisfied
One cannot remember the day there was want
The sweetness and light arouse sublime splendor
That ripples through matter, making it dissolve

No longer flesh and bone, but electric fire and light
Vibration so intense yet subtle
How does man describe ecstacy?

Words do not do justice to this ultimate romance

Where love meets soul with no separation
Fleshly pleasures wane
The heart expands to fill the universe in exquisite,
intimate union.

He Has Me

That Voice called to my soul and would not halt its calling

That flame draws the moth to itself, ignoring all former ties

The One Tie, the one, inseparable connection placed before matter took on form

The primary union forgotten but not gone

His Voice awakens a remembrance beyond reason. I fly toward it.

Things, people, fall away as the tractor beam of Truth pulls me to Itself

It is beyond will, beyond desire, this annihilating force,

Which strips me of all life, all breath, save His own which sustains me

My senses have the taste for Him alone, all other pleasures lose their savor

This urgent passion draws me deeper, bereft of a resting place save His Heart.

He is a jealous lover. He would have me completely.

Quiet hours

In quiet hours
I remember you to my Lord
You who suffer and are sorrowful
You who are sick and dying
You who grieve
In quiet hours
I pour out my heart
To my sweet, benevolent Christ
To comfort and strengthen and spare you
To lift you up and hold you
In tender arms
And moreso still for those who seem complete
Whose lives look good, but whose hearts weep
The silent tears of loneliness
Of prideful hearts too hard to break
For fear of crumbling into dust
Erased by wind

And so these quiet hours go
Conversing with my God who knows
The deep desire of my heart
For all to know what He doth brought
The solace of the wretched
Salvation's peace

Rev. Mary Francis Drake, MA, MSW, is an ordained minister, University faculty member, Hospice Chaplain and mother of 3. She resides in New Hampshire where she offers spiritual teaching and counseling at the Pure Life Meditation Center and Grace Chapel. This is Rev. Mary Francis' first attempt at publishing her mystical poetry and universal spiritual teachings in her voice and through her heart. She genuinely hopes you find it both inspiring and helpful in your journey.

Peace to all, and love.